**Books are to be returned on or before
the last date below.**

Exhibition
CATALOGUE

Salvatore Ferragamo EVOLVING LEGEND 1928-2008

菲拉格慕－不朽的传奇

SKIRA

Design
Studio Contri Toscano

Editing
Emanuela Di Lallo
Raffaella Gallio

Translations
Christopher Shanti Evans, Raffaella
Gallio, Cecilia Ma, Marco Migotto
for Language Consulting Congressi,
Milano
Steve Chaplin

First published in Italy in 2008
by Skira Editore S.p.A.
Palazzo Casati Stampa
via Torino 61
20123 Milano
Italy
www.skira.net

Printed and bound in Italy.
First edition

ISBN: 978-88-6130-616-5

Distributed in North America by
Rizzoli International Publications, Inc.,
300 Park Avenue South, New York, NY
10010, USA.
Distributed elsewhere in the world by
Thames and Hudson Ltd., 181A High
Holborn, London WC1V 7QX, United
Kingdom.

美术设计
Studio Contri Toscano

编辑
Emanuela Di Lallo
Raffaella Gallio

翻译
Raffaella Gallio、Christopher Shanti
Evans、Marco Migotto、马思涵为
意大利米兰Language Consulting
Congressi
Steve Chaplin

2008年于意大利首版
Skira Editore S.p.A.出版
Palazzo Casati Stampa
via Torino 61
20123 Milano
Italy
www.skira.net

ISBN: 978-88-6130-616-5

由Rizzoli国际出版公司在北美发行；
公司地址：300 Park Avenue South,
New York, NY 10010, USA
由Thames and Hudson有限公司在
世界其他国家和地区经销；
公司地址：181A High Holborn,
London, WC1V 7QX, United Kingdom

Salvatore Ferragamo EVOLVING LEGEND 1928-2008

菲拉格慕－不朽的传奇

Shanghai
Museum of Contemporary Art
29 March – 7 May 2008

Exhibition promoted and organised by
Museo Salvatore Ferragamo
and MoCA, Shanghai

Patrons
Italian Embassy in Beijing
Italian Trade Commission
Italian Consulate in Shanghai

上海
当代艺术馆
2008年3月29日 – 5月7日

展览促进和组织单位
萨尔瓦托勒·菲拉格慕博物馆
上海当代艺术馆

协办单位
意大利驻北京大使馆
意大利对外贸易委员会
意大利驻上海领事馆

Museo Salvatore Ferragamo

Director
Stefania Ricci

Catalogue edited by
Stefania Ricci

Exhibition curated by
Cristina Morozzi
Stefania Ricci
With the collaboration of
Museum of Contemporary Art
(MoCA), Shanghai

Production designer
Studio RBA

Exhibition set up
Melaverde

Insurance
Aon S.p.A.

萨尔瓦托勒·菲拉格慕博物馆

馆长
Stefania Ricci

主编
Stefania Ricci

展览协调
Cristina Morozzi
Stefania Ricci
会同
上海当代艺术馆

策划
Studio RBA

布展
Melaverde

保险
Aon S.p.A.

Istituto nazionale per il Commercio Estero
意大利对外贸易委员会
Italian Trade Commission

Photo and film credits

Archivi Alinari, Florence
Archivio Corbis, Milan
Archivio Farabola, Milan
Archivio Grazia Neri, Milan
Archivio Museo Salvatore Ferragamo,
Florence
Archivio Storico del Cinema Afe
di Pietro Servo, Rome
Archivio Storico Foto Locchi, Florence
A R Media
Giampaolo Barbieri
Vanessa Beecroft
Stefano Biliotti
Brigham Young University, Cecil
B. De Mille Archive, Provo (Utah)
Christopher Broadbent
Marco Cardelli
Creative Business
Patrick De Marchelier
Guglielmo De Micheli
Eldorado
Aldo Fallai
Fabrizio Ferri
Paolo Gandola
Giovanni Gastel
Giovanni Giannoni
Allan Grant
Dominique Issermann
Istituto Luce, Rome
David Lees
François Matthys
Meldolesi
Sergio Merli
Daniel Meyer
Paul Getty Images
Stefano Peruzy
Roberto Quagli
André Rau
Robert Stigwood, Andrew G. Vajna
Production
Roli Collection (by courtesy
of Amin Jaffer Editor)
Studio Poli
Mario Testino
Time-Life Syndication, New York
The Academy of Motion Pictures Arts
and Sciences, Los Angeles
The Kobal Collection, London
Eric Traore
Twentieth Century Fox

The Museo Salvatore Ferragamo is at
the disposal of the copyright holders
of images from unidentified sources

The authors wish to thank

Cristina Acidini Luchinat, Head
of the Soprintendenza del Polo
Museale Fiorentino; Marta Bencini,
Secretary of the Soprintendenza
del Polo Museale Fiorentino; Elsa
Benitez; Daniela Cecchini, Servizio
Secondo alla Direzione Generale del
Ministero dei Beni Artistici e Storici in
Rome; Katrina Chang, CEO of MoCA,
Shanghai; Pierluigi Finotello, Museo
di Storia Naturale - Zoologica
"La Specola"; Maurizio Forte,
Director, Italian Trade Commission,
Shanghai; Giuseppe Guliza, Fine Arts
and Antiques Export Office,
Soprintendenza Speciale per
il Patrimonio Storico, Artistico
ed Etnoantropologico e per il Polo
Museale della Città di Firenze;
Samuel Kung, Chairman and Director
of MoCA in Shanghai; Victoria Lu,
Creative Director of MoCA in
Shanghai; Franca Pinzauti; Bruno
Santi, Head of the Soprintendenza
per i Beni Artistici e Storici delle
Province di Firenze, Pistoia e Prato;
Claudia Schiffer; Riccardo Sessa,
Italian Ambassador in Beijing;
Umberto Vattani, President of the
Italian Trade Commission

The authors also wish to thank

Timex
Luxottica

图片和胶片提供

佛罗伦萨Alinari公司摄影档案处
米兰Corbis公司摄影档案处
米兰Farabola公司摄影档案处
米兰Grazia Neri公司摄影档案处
佛罗伦萨萨尔瓦托勒·菲拉格慕博物馆
档案处
罗马Afe di Pietro Servo公司电影历史
档案处
佛罗伦萨Locchi公司摄影历史档案处
A R Media
Vanessa Beecroft
Giampaolo Barbieri
Stefano Biliotti
Brigham Young University, Cecil
B. De Mille公司电影历史档案处
Christopher Broadbent
Marco Cardelli
Creative Business
Patrick De Marchelier
Guglielmo De Micheli
Eldorado
Aldo Fallai
Fabrizio Ferri
Paolo Gandola
Giovanni Gastel
Giovanni Giannoni
Allan Grant
Dominique Issermann
罗马Istituto Luce
David Lees
François Matthys
Meldolesi
Sergio Merli
Daniel Meyer
Paul Getty Images
Stefano Peruzy
Roberto Quagli
André Rau
Robert Stigwood、Andrew G. Vajna
电影制片
Roli Collection（由Amin Jaffer提供）
Studio Poli
Mario Testino
纽约Time-Life Syndication
洛杉矶The Academy of Motion
Pictures Arts and Sciences
伦敦The Kobal Collection
Eric Traore
Twentieth Century Fox

萨尔瓦托勒·菲拉格慕博物馆对不明来
源的图片听候版权所有者的处置建议。

作者希望感谢：

佛罗伦萨博物馆管理局负责人Cristina
Acidini Luchinat；佛罗伦萨博物馆管
理局秘书处负责人Marta Bencini；Elsa
Benitez；意大利文化部艺术和历史司
二处Daniela Cecchini；La Specola自
然-动物博物馆Pierluigi Finotello；意
大利外贸委员会上海代表处首席代表
Maurizio Forte；佛罗伦萨博物馆管理
局历史、艺术和人类遗产特别管理处文
物和艺术品出口处Giuseppe Guliza；
上海当代艺术馆主席兼馆长龚明光；上
海当代艺术馆创意总监陆蓉之；Franca
Pinzauti；佛罗伦萨、比斯托亚和普拉
托三省历史与艺术遗产管理局负责人
Bruno Santi；Claudia Schiffer；意大
利驻北京大使Riccardo Sessa；意大利
对外贸易委员会主席Umberto Vattani；
艺术馆首席执行官张戎谊。

另外，作者还希望感谢：

Timex
Luxottica

Contents 目录

Foreword

My family and I decided to celebrate the eighty-year anniversary of our company in Shanghai, China – a country with a thousand-year-old tradition – and in a prestigious museum, the MoCA. In reality, the Ferragamo name has been known to the fashion world for almost one hundred years. My husband Salvatore made the name famous in California, first in Santa Barbara and then in Hollywood, creating footwear for the most beautiful women in the world – the "divas" of emerging American cinema.

The event has such meaning for us that for the first time we decided to present a retrospective show not on the history of Salvatore the man but on the company he founded: its identity, inventions and the values it was shaped by.

It is important to make known that Salvatore Ferragamo and his company based their work not only on the creativity of products but mainly on the concept of service to others. My husband developed shoe criteria based on the foot's anatomy from studying at the University of California in the United States in the 1920s; the shoes he developed aimed to give the body stability and enable it to walk properly. These principles have been further developed by the present company and translated into every sector, so that the care and attention to detail brought to shoes would be transferred to other products.

I would like to thank all those who helped make this project a success: the Chinese authorities, the Italian Embassy and MoCA management, who made the event possible; the journalists who supported it and whom I thank for their presence; and the curators and architects who set up the exhibition, confirming yet again the collaborative relationship which has always existed between Ferragamo and this marvellous country, whose future development is in no doubt.

Wanda Ferragamo
Honorary Chairman, Salvatore Ferragamo Italia S.p.A.

序言

我和我的家族决定在中国，这个拥有着数千年悠久历史的国度举办我们的公司创建80周年庆典，地点选择于著名的博物馆——上海当代艺术馆。事实上，菲拉格慕品牌在时尚界享有显赫声誉已近百年。是我的丈夫萨尔瓦托勒在加利福尼亚使之声名远扬。他先是在圣巴巴拉市，后来是在好莱坞为世界上最美丽的女性和正在兴起的美国电影业的女神们制作鞋履。

此次活动对于我们来说意义非同寻常，因为此次回顾展将首次不以萨尔瓦托勒本人的经历为主题，而是旨在呈献他所创建公司的发展历程，及其独特的风格、众多的创新和它赖以发展的价值与理念。

萨尔瓦托勒·菲拉格慕和公司所取得的成就，不仅建立于非凡的产品创造力之上，而更在于竭诚为他人服务的理念之上，将此展示于众非常重要。我丈夫早在20年代在美国研发的制鞋标准就是基于他在加州大学学习的脚部解剖学，这一标准旨在为身体带来良好的平稳性，使行走变得舒适惬意。当今公司进一步发展了这些准则，并将其延伸到每一个领域，将制鞋中对细节的关注和悉心拓展到公司的其它产品之上。

在此，我要感谢所有为这个项目的成功而付出努力的人们，感谢使项目得以实施的中国政府部门、意大利大使馆、当代艺术馆的领导，以及予以支持的记者朋友们，对他们的出席我深表谢意；我要感谢协助展览陈列的策划人员和建筑师们，他们使展览成为菲拉格慕和这个神奇国家之间一直以来良好合作的见证。我们对中国未来的发展深信不疑。

蔓达·菲拉格慕

意大利萨尔瓦托勒·菲拉格慕公司名誉主席

Preface

Since the Renaissance, Italy has been a country of culture and art. With historic relics and cultural heritage spreading all over the peninsula serving as a source of inspiration for many designers, Italy is historically bound to become a power in fashion. The land has been the birthplace of numerous professional talents, creating countless occasions of contingency and keeping Italy's fashion industry in a leading position and at its peak. In recent years, more and more top brands are integrating arts into their design of luxury items through multi-media across different domains, infusing amazingly diversified features into industrial products.

Italy's fashion industry emerged out of the shadows of the Second World War in the 1950s. Fashion shows in Rome and Florence soon became the most spectacular events in the international fashion community. By the 1970s, Milan as a new force had also gained the leading status in the world of fashion. "Made in Italy" luxury brands have since been the pursuit of fashion elites.

Tracing back to the 1920s, the art of Ferragamo shoemaking already emerged in the West as a symbol of "Made in Italy" luxury. Mr Salvatore Ferragamo, renowned for his shoemaking techniques, devoted his lifetime to researching for and making fit and comfortable shoes. His inherent sense of aesthetics was brought into full play in shoe design. With his artistic talents, he also changed the history of shoemaking. His never-failing originality, elaborate techniques, exquisite and unparalleled design, as well as the use of the finest materials, reflected innovative design concepts right on the pulse of the times. Moreover, his cross-domain cooperation with other artists brought his creativity in shoe design up to the level of art. Today, Ferragamo's shoes are simply regarded as exquisite works of art made in Italy.

Craftsmanship and innovation are the two important factors that differentiate one fashion brand from another. Italy's fashion industry is the best essence extracted from aesthetics in daily life and is vigorously promoted to the world by Italy's government institutions. After the *Italy Made in Art: Now* exhibition staged in 2006, driven by Italian Trade Commission, MoCA Shanghai has once again become the gorgeous stage to showcase the charm of Italian culture in China on the occasion of Ferragamo's eightieth anniversary and for Ferragamo's global celebration in China. The famous Italian exhibition curator Stefania Ricci has offered a magnificent selection of shoes and fashion works embodying social and cultural changes over time, and has organised a grand international exhibition focusing on Italy's shoemaking design and its course of development.

Since its founding, MoCA Shanghai has been upholding innovation as its core value. Our cooperation with the fashion industry aims to create an additional image of museum culture to the outside world. It is our anticipation that visitors will get a closer view of the Ferragamo design concept, representing the beauty of Italian craftsmanship and reflecting the history of creative development in fashion. The exhibition would not have been possible without the contribution of many. I would like to thank Mrs Wanda Ferragamo and her family; Umberto Vattani, Chairman of Italian Trade Commission and Maurizio Forte, Trade Commissioner of its Shanghai office; as well as Stefania Ricci, the exhibition curator. I would also like to thank the entire team from Italy and our own colleagues of MoCA Shanghai, for their joint efforts. Most of all, I wish an enormous success for the exhibition as part of the celebration for Ferragamo's eightieth anniversary.

Samuel Kung
Chairman and Director of MoCA Shanghai

引言

意大利自文艺复兴时代以来,一直是以文化、艺术立国。半岛上处处可见的古迹、大量的文化遗产，经常是许多设计师寻找灵感的泉源。意大利成为一个时尚大国，是历史的必然;而在这块土地上孕育的许多杰出人才，则创造了无数的偶然，使意大利的时尚产业保持在领先和巅峰的状态。近些年来，越来越多顶级品牌更以跨领域的媒介手法，将艺术融入在奢华产品的设计之中，为刻板的工业产品注入了令人惊艳的丰富面貌。

上一世纪50年代，意大利的服饰、时尚产业，走出第二次世界大战的阴影，罗马和佛罗伦萨两地的时装秀成为国际间圈内人士最受瞩目的盛事。到了70年代，米兰更异军突起，成为世界时装工业的重镇。"意大利制造"的奢华品牌，从此成为时尚精英追捧的对象。

追溯回上一世纪20年代，菲拉格慕(Ferragamo)制鞋的艺术，便已经在西方社会崭露头角，可说是"意大利制造"奢华品牌的代表者。以制鞋闻名天下的萨尔瓦托勒·菲拉格慕先生，一生致力研究制作合脚舒适的鞋品，以其与生俱来的审美品位，在设计鞋履方面施展身手。他这种艺术家的天赋，改变了制鞋业的历史，他源源不绝的创意、格外讲究的工艺、精妙绝伦的设计和顶级的选材，反映了一位设计师紧贴时代脉搏的创意概念。他与其他艺术家的跨领域合作，更将鞋履的创作提升至艺术的殿堂。在今天看来，菲拉格慕的鞋子，就代表了意大利制作的精美艺术品。

工艺与创新，是促使时尚品牌卓尔不凡的两个重要因素。意大利的时尚产业，其实就是从生活美学中萃取出的极品精华，意大利政府也经常将意大利的时尚文化推广到全世界。继本馆2006年推出《意大利制造之艺术：今日》展览之后，今年欣逢菲拉格慕创业80周年，在意大利对外贸易委员会的推动下，上海当代艺术馆再一次成为意大利文化到中国展现风姿的亮丽舞台，是菲拉格慕全球庆祝活动的中国站点。来自意大利的著名策展人斯蒂凡娅·瑞奇(Stefania Ricci)，精选了蕴涵着社会发展脚步和文化的鞋履与时尚服饰作品，组织了一场演绎意大利鞋艺设计和发展历程为中心的国际大展。

上海当代艺术馆自创馆以来，便以创新为核心理念。跨领域与时尚圈的越界合作，也是本馆为艺术馆文化向外推动一番新气象的尝试。我希望观众在精心设计的时光隧道展场穿梭漫步时，能够近距离欣赏代表意大利时尚工艺之美的菲拉格慕设计理念。而这次展出活动得以顺利推出，在此我要感谢蔓达·菲拉格慕夫人(Mrs. Wanda Ferragamo)及其家族成员，意大利对外贸易委员会主席Umberto Vattani，上海代表处首席代表Maurizio Forte，策展人斯蒂凡娅·瑞奇，意大利相关工作人员和本馆的全体同仁一起付出的努力，并祝愿菲拉格慕创业80周年回顾展能够圆满成功。

龚明光

上海当代艺术馆主席兼馆长

Stefania Ricci Salvatore Ferragamo: An Evolving Legend

There are people whose exceptional individual gifts have turned their lives into legends, and whose professional and private stories are worth telling to show just what is possible. Salvatore Ferragamo is one of these.

Salvatore was born in 1898 at Bonito in the province of Avellino, a small town in the South of Italy, with the vocation to be a shoemaker. He made very rapid progress in his career. At the age of nine he realised his first pair of shoes for his sister's First Communion and began an apprenticeship with the local shoemaker. By the time he was eleven he had a small workshop of his own where he created fine models for the wealthy ladies of the town. Loath to settle for what he had already achieved, however, just as was to happen many other times over the course of his life, he decided to complete his professional training in Naples, where the handcrafting of footwear had attained levels of excellence.

By the age of sixteen Salvatore had learnt everything there was to learn in Italy about the art of shoemaking and consequently, driven once again by his thirst for knowledge, decided to join his older brothers in the United States, where the shoe industry had begun its life only a few years earlier.

Landing in New York, he moved to Boston and found a job in a shoe factory. But the experience proved a disappointment. Salvatore was impressed by the efficiency of the American industry, but not by the end result. He found the mass-produced shoes to be of fairly good quality in comparison with the average American production, but heavy and clumsy in their style and construction when compared with the ones that any good shoemaker could have turned out back home in Italy.

So Salvatore persuaded his brothers to move to the West Coast, to the city of Santa Barbara where the movie industry was coming into being and where he saw good

Salvatore Ferragamo
looking through the vinyl
sole of one of his famous
shoes. 1955.

Bonito at the beginning
of the twentieth century.

萨尔瓦托勒·菲拉格慕透
过一款乙烯树脂鞋底望
出，此鞋款是他最著名的
创作之一。1955年。

20世纪初的博尼托。

The American factory
producing *Queen Quality*
footwear where Salvatore
Ferragamo worked for a
fortnight after his arrival
in the United States.

生产"女皇品质"鞋履
的美国工厂，萨尔瓦托
勒·菲拉格慕抵达美国后
曾在此工作过两个星期。

Customers in the Hollywood Boot Shop.

The official announcement of the opening of the Hollywood Boot Shop from the 20 April 1923 edition of *Holly Leaves*.

顾客光顾好莱坞鞋店。

好莱坞鞋店于1923年4月20日开业的正式告示，Holly Leaves 版。

prospects of success for luxury shoes, crafted entirely by hand, like the ones that the skilled Italian cobbler was capable of making. He opened a small shop for the repair and manufacture of shoes to measure and in the evening attended courses in the anatomy of the foot at the local university, prompted by the desire to create shoes that would not only be beautiful but also comfortable and practical, a goal that had obsessed him from the outset. These years were to prove fundamental to his development and to the creation of the Ferragamo fit, to which the name owes much of its fame and which, after the founder's death in 1960, would be applied to mass production, becoming a mark of the brand's identity.

The opportunity to make himself known was provided by the American Film Company with a first order for a consignment of cowboy boots. From that moment on his reputation grew among the directors and stars of silent cinema. His most regular customers were Pola Negri, Mary Pickford and her sister Lottie, Gloria Swanson and Mae West, who all began to wear Ferragamo shoes even off set. Ferragamo specialised chiefly in women's shoes, although he did make models for men, produced for a number of films and for friends like Rodolfo Valentino. When the movie industry moved to Hollywood in 1923, Salvatore went with it and opened a new, elegant and spacious store, the Hollywood Boot Shop, located on one of the main streets of Beverly Hills, Hollywood Boulevard, on the corner with Las Palmas. Directors like Cecil De Mille, James Cruze, David Wark Griffith and Raoul Walsh commissioned the footwear for their costume pictures from Ferragamo. Actresses competed for his eccentric models, in which the young Salvatore was able to give full play to his creative imagination and his passion for experimentation with techniques and materials, something to which the strong demand of the market for women's footwear had contributed.

Yet orders, which were boosted by collaboration with the first American department stores, Saks in New York and I. Magnin in San Francisco, were often left unfulfilled owing to the difficulty of finding skilled labour capable of making shoes by hand in the United States.

In 1927, in search of qualified craftsmen, Ferragamo decided to go back to Italy and chose as the new base for his activity Florence, a city and a region known and appreciated all over the world for the beauty of its art and the refinement of its handicrafts. In Florence he found the ideal terrain to develop his fanciful inventiveness and build on the contemporary myth of the Renaissance workshop, the place where artists were trained, where ideas were born, where masterpieces were created. He realised the power of a message that coupled a high-quality handcrafted product

Announcing

That Salvatore Farragamo has bought the Hollywood Boot Shop from J. M. Bohannon and will run it under the same high-class management which proved so successful in his Santa Barbara shop for the last seven years.

Hollywood Boot Shop
6687 Hollywood Blvd.
577-101

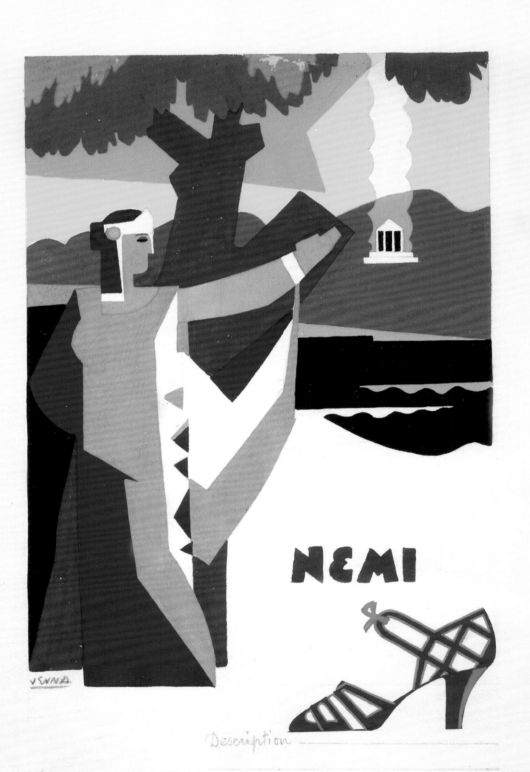

with the image of such a unique place and that fostered in the mind of his customers, especially the foreign ones, the illusion that possessing a Ferragamo shoe was like owning a piece of Florence, of its art and its cultural tradition.

In Florence he decided to set up his first real company, Salvatore Ferragamo, and his name became synonymous with a brand.

He brought to that fertile ground a wave of innovation, the product of his experience overseas. He transferred the manufacturing process of the American footwear industry to manual production, creating a human assembly line in which the shoemaker became the expert at a specific stage of the work. He also introduced into his production the American system of sizes, which allowed for a wide variety of numbers corresponding not just to the different lengths of the foot but also to its different widths, making his own adjustments to it. He invented new technical solutions, such as a steel middle sole to support the arch of the foot. Over the years he patented a series of structural innovations that set trends: from complete freedom to experimentation with materials, which he adopted right across the range, from the finest and most expensive to the latest inventions and the more traditional types. These last were totally transformed by the uncommon use to which they were put, by unexpected combinations of colours and decorations, like straw plaits of the kind used on hats which became uppers for refined models, or lace from Tavarnelle

Salvatore Ferragamo
creating a shoe directly
on the customer's foot.

Palazzo Spini
Feroni, Ferragamo's
headquarters from 1938.

萨尔瓦托勒·菲拉格慕为
顾客现场创作鞋履。

佛罗伦萨费罗尼 – 斯皮尼
大宅（Spini Feroni），
1938年成为菲拉格慕的
总部。

which, thanks to Ferragamo, found new fields of application. A man of his time, he did not remain indifferent to contemporary art. He employed an artist, Lucio Venna, an exponent of Futurism, to design his first advertising campaigns and the logo to be printed on the label of the shoes. As one of the great industrial designers of the age, he invented forms on the basis of functional requirements that suggested the appearance. He created unique and exclusive pieces, which resembled *objets d'art* in their refinement and the care taken over details, and at the same time he patented every one of his ideas that had potential for mass production, facing up squarely to the problem of industrialisation. Almost four hundred patents covering ornamentation, practical improvements, inventions and commercial aspects have recently been tracked down at the State Archives in Rome and document the marriage of an unbounded creative energy with a mastery of the technique of construction over the entire span of his career.

His creations of the late 1920s and early 1930s stand out for the decoration of the uppers and for their strong and decided tones of colour, which he used in uncommon and bold combinations in his patchworks of fabrics and hides. In the uppers sinuous and curved lines were coupled with geometric patterns, inspired by the abstract art of the period. At the same time Ferragamo drew adroitly on the whole spectrum of the Florentine craft tradition, ranging from magnificent architectural decorations in wrought iron to small mosaics produced by local goldsmiths, and alternated them with motifs of Classical or Oriental flavour.

If on the one hand Ferragamo studied exclusive ornamental forms, through which he achieved a customisation of the object, on the other he paid attention to the functionality of the product.

However, poor management and the economic crisis that followed the fall in the value of the dollar in 1929 forced Ferragamo to interrupt his creative production and close down his first workshop at Via Mannelli 57 in 1933. Undiscouraged, he rented new premises in the heart of Florence, at Palazzo Spini Feroni in Via Tornabuoni, and resumed work and his activity of exportation to the United States with even more energy and enthusiasm than before, trying not to repeat the mistakes he had made previously and to make a name for himself with the local and European clientele. His revival was a rapid one and by 1938 Salvatore was in a position to buy the building, where he had installed the workshop on the first floor and the store on the ground floor. The same year he opened two branches, one in Old Bond Street in London and another in Via Condotti in Rome.

In these years every shoe that Ferragamo designed was almost a work of architecture, in the construction of its details, in its symmetries, in the perfect balancing of weights and measurements. The wedge heel made of cork was perhaps the most celebrated of Ferragamo's inventions of the period. It was patented in 1937, at least two years before it became all the rage in international fashion and a hallmark of the taste of the time. It was originally developed to meet a functional need, that of raising the heel and giving the arch of the foot a stable support while solving in a brilliant and imaginative way a problem that had arisen at the start of the war in Ethiopia, when the economic sanctions imposed on Italy by the League of Nations had affected, among other imported materials, the German steel that Ferragamo used to make his metal middle soles. The wedge offered an artist like him the opportunity to give rein to his creative imagination on surfaces of greater size than those provided by uppers and heels.

Sandal with cylindrical heel in transparent Bakelite. 1939.

Sandal platform covered with hand-painted satin in Chinese style. 1938.

柱形透明树脂高跟凉鞋，1939年。

厚底凉鞋，外包中式风格手工绘画绸缎，1938年。

The economic sanctions imposed on Italy, which had aggravated the problems linked to the country's shortage of material and energy resources, stimulated Ferragamo's inventiveness not only in the area of ornamentation but also in that of technology. He designed heels that were made by stitching together the corks of wine bottles and then covering them with leather and patented special procedures for the preparation of substitutes for leather. He invented heels of transparent Bakelite and jointed wood soles, with uppers made of Galalith or decorated with glass, imitating the wheels of cars or reels of sewing thread.

His natural inclination towards humble materials, as a demonstration that luxury does not depend on the value of the material employed but on the idea and the quality of the workmanship, led him from the early 1930s onwards to make extensive use of fabrics made from hemp, straw, woollen thread and cellophane produced from sweet wrappers, which formed shiny, thick and pleated surfaces.

Even before the international jet set developed a fondness for Florence in the 1950s, Ferragamo established personal relationships with a number of celebrities, including queens, aristocrats and actresses, who came in person to the frescoed rooms of Palazzo Spini Feroni to have him take the measurements of their feet and to hear his latest suggestions about what they should wear on them.

The re-opening of frontiers at the end of the war and the resumption of trade marked the beginning of a particularly fertile period for Ferragamo and for Italian design as a whole, ready to take off in a big way and to receive the appreciation it deserved

from critics and the market at an international level. Salvatore Ferragamo became an illustrious spokesman for Italian fantasy and style in fashion. In 1947 he devised an upper made of transparent nylon filament yarn and used it to create the "invisible" sandal with which he won the Neiman Marcus Award in Dallas, the "Oscar of Fashion", along with Christian Dior.

In the second half of the 1950s Ferragamo started to think about the future and how to deal with the growing competitiveness and exacting demands of international markets.

In less than ten years, industrial activity in Italy had attained unprecedented levels, growing at a rate superior to that of any other country in Europe. The political alliance with the United States had brought with it an economic partnership that in practice had translated into the sale of American machinery, industrial equipment and patents to the Old World. The spread of industrialisation had resulted in a progressive democratisation of consumer goods, while the cost of labour, still low when compared with that of other European countries, had made it possible to keep prices stable and Italian products became increasingly competitive on the international market.

Thus the transformation of the Italian economy, the appearance of new footwear manufacturers and brands on the international market and the growth in domestic demand induced Salvatore Ferragamo to reconsider his strategy of production. In 1948 he had turned down an offer of 50,000 dollars a year over a period of twenty years from an American factory for the use of the *Ferragamo Debs* brand in one of its industrial lines of shoes. But ten years later he was obliged to make a compromise if he wanted Ferragamo footwear to preserve its position in the market and increase its turnover. While continuing to produce some shoes by hand, Ferragamo designed a couple of secondary and less expensive lines, *Ferragamo Debs* and *Ferrina Shoes*, that were made in England, 60% still by hand and 40% by machine. At the same time he began to diversify the range of his products, creating his first bags, printing silk scarves with motifs inspired by the principal Italian cities and their artistic treasures and, in 1959, lending his name to a collection of sportswear for Lord and Taylor, designed by his second daughter, Giovanna.

In 1960 Salvatore died and the management of the business was taken over by his wife Wanda and six children, each of whom was assigned a clearly defined role.

For the next ten years, Salvatore Ferragamo was a company run by women. Wanda, who up until then had stuck to the role of wife and mother, found herself overseeing the difficult transition from a small firm, focused on a niche market, to a large company whose products were sold in thirty-five different countries. Giovanna continued to develop her women's ready-to-wear in collections that were ever more complete, earning herself the full right to participate in the shows of Italian fashion held at the prestigious venue of Florence's Palazzo Pitti from 1965 onwards.

Fiamma, the eldest daughter and the only one of the six children to have worked in close contact with their father, was given responsibility for the creative direction of the footwear sector and took the important decision to move from artisan to industrial production, retaining only a few manual stages in the manufacturing process. The shift appeared necessary if the company was going to expand its distribution and achieve competitive prices, while preserving the characteristics of the luxury product. "I loved studying art, literature, music", recounted Fiamma, "and I had no intention of giving up my studies. But my father was convinced that my future lay

Il Mattino dell'Italia centrale. 1947.

A drawing by Maria Pezzi in the renowned *Bellezza* magazine characterises Salvatore Ferragamo as the shoemaker to the stars. 1950s.

摘自《意大利中央晨报》，1947年。

二十世纪50年代玛丽亚·佩兹（Maria Pezzi）为著名的《Bellezza》杂志创作的绘画，由此萨尔瓦托勒·菲拉格慕被誉为"明星御用之鞋匠"。

in the company. And in the end he managed to persuade me. In the early days I tried to keep a foot in both camps, working and studying, but the work fascinated me more and more every day until I reached the point where the choice became definitive. I knew nothing about shoes, but my father was always at my side, encouraging me, teaching me how to choose materials, to understand the quality of the workmanship, to come up with the right models for the fashion of the moment. He was a very strict man, but considerate at the same time. Not just with me but with his shoemakers too. If one of them made a mistake, he found a way to mention his merits first, and then took him to task."

On her father's death, Fiamma had to confront the market's initial lack of confidence in the potential of the brand beyond Salvatore. In January 1961 she went to London to present her first collection and to her great surprise the response of the buyers was not just positive but enthusiastic. "They asked me", Fiamma went on, "if any of the designs were my father's. I told them we had so many models in the archives that had been designed by him but not produced that I would be able to live off them for years. This answer was sufficient to reassure them. The orders came in. I had achieved what I wanted, winning their confidence and guaranteeing the con-

The first ever Italian fashion show took place in Florence in 1951, featuring Ferragamo's *Kimo.*

1951年在佛罗伦萨举办的首届意大利时装展，菲拉格慕的"Kimo"女鞋参加了展出。

Left to right

Giovanna Ferragamo
with her father Salvatore
in 1959.

Wanda and Salvatore
Ferragamo with Christian
Dior in Florence in 1949.

Leonardo Ferragamo
with his parents in 1954.

Wanda and Salvatore
Ferragamo in 1947.

Fiamma and Giovanna
Ferragamo in 1963.

Fiamma Ferragamo
at work in 1966.

（从左到右）

乔瓦娜·菲拉格慕与父亲
萨尔瓦托勒，1959年。

萨尔瓦托勒、蔓达·菲拉
格慕夫妇与克里司汀·迪
奥（Christian Dior）在佛
罗伦萨，1949年。

莱昂纳多·菲拉格慕与父
母，1954年。

蔓达与萨尔瓦托勒·菲拉
格慕，1947年。

菲安玛和乔瓦娜·菲拉格
慕，1963年。

工作中的菲安玛·菲拉格
慕，1966年。

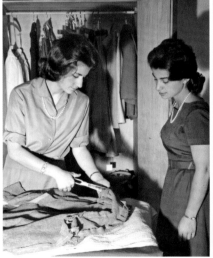

tinuity of the tradition." Each season the two sisters, Fiamma and Giovanna, the "teenagers of fashion" as they were dubbed by the press, showed their collections in Italy, London and the United States, where Ferragamo had set up a company for distributing his products in North America in the 1950s. In the morning and afternoon they presented their models to buyers; in the evening they went to sleep at a convent because their mother Wanda did not think it proper for two young women to stay in a hotel.

In the 1960s the effects of the economic boom of the previous decade became a tangible reality, generating enthusiasm for industrial progress, seen as the dispenser of prosperity. Even the highest segment of the market, that of luxury goods, increased its share. From the elite of consumers, which was still the target of reference in the 1950s, attention shifted to the lower middle class, which wanted to demonstrate its social respectability through the use and the image of a distinctive product, be it a car or a pair of shoes. In fact it is no coincidence that this period saw the establishment of the name and logo of a designer as an element guaranteeing the quality and recognisability of a product. The immediate effect of this at Ferragamo was the decision to change the logo. The name "Ferragamo's Creations", used as the label for the shoes until the 1950s, was replaced by a graphic rendering of the founder's signature which, in an effort to keep his creative identity alive, was utilised to brand the products, the signs of the stores, the packaging and the advertising.

There were two different reactions to the new trend in the market among manufacturers. Some lowered the level of quality, favouring mass production, while others, like Ferragamo, which had a tradition and a prestigious brand to defend, decided to widen the gap between mid-level production and that of high quality, for which they were famous, rendering their products exclusive and targeting them at a select clientele. On the one hand Ferragamo continued to create high-fashion and made-to-measure shoes based on the craftsmanship and the principles of excellence that had made the brand's name, turning each model into what was almost a one-off piece, an icon of style. On the other, it developed the mass-produced collection that accompanied ready-to-wear, transferring to it the care over detail and the quality of the materials that characterised its top line. Over the course of the decade the production of made-to-measure shoes gradually declined as the company came to focus on an ever wider international distribution and on the diversification of its products, such as bags, which it began to produce on a regular basis in 1965.

Great attention was paid to maintaining Salvatore's emphasis on the fit and comfortableness of the shoes, without neglecting the aesthetics of the product.

Within a short time the internal organisation of the company was modified as well. While in the 1950s the daily production was 350 pairs of shoes, made by hand by its own workforce of 750 craftsmen, in the 1960s this rose to 2000 pairs, made in small factories in the Neapolitan region and in the industrial areas close to Florence which worked exclusively for Ferragamo. The creative part and the construction of the prototypes and lasts, on which the fit of the shoes depended, remained within the company. In 1964 the oldest of Salvatore's sons, Ferruccio, joined the firm in a management role, and he was followed in the 1970s by his sister Fulvia, placed in charge of the design and production of silk accessories, scarves, ties and gifts, and his brother Leonardo, who set up the men's-wear sector of Ferragamo, producing clothing and accessories, and was subsequently responsible for the company's huge expansion in the Far East. The last in order of time to join the family firm was

Models by Giovanna Ferragamo at Forte Belvedere in 1962.

收藏于佛罗伦萨Forte Belvedere的乔瓦娜·菲拉格慕设计的鞋款，1962年。

the youngest brother Massimo, on whom fell the demanding task of handling the US market, which has always been the most important and profitable for Ferragamo. While building on the founding principles of the brand, Wanda and her children have had the merit of making the best of the difficult creative legacy left by Salvatore. In the absence of the great designer, who had revolutionised the history of footwear with his models and his ideas, they have focused on a metropolitan style, where design is combined with the quality of the hides and the workmanship, with attention to detail and with innovation in materials, in line with the company tradition. If Ferragamo's production in Salvatore's time was rooted in the originality of the models, in continual innovation and, at times, in eccentricity, since his passing it has been based on a measured elegance, capable of meeting the demands of a much broader market, and one which caters to different cultures of dress.

This does not mean that there has no longer been room for invention and experimentation. Among the company's many patents, which range from nonslip soles to briefcases in carbon fibre, it is certainly worth mentioning the spiral heel and sculpture heel that earned Fiamma the Neiman Marcus Award for creativity in footwear, twenty years after her father, and above all the two most celebrated symbols of the Ferragamo of today: *Vara*, a court shoe with a bow that was invented in 1978 and is still on sale today without any great changes, and *Gancino*, the ornament that was born as the clasp of a bag designed by Salvatore, to judge by a blurred photograph from the 1950s, but that was undoubtedly made famous all over the world by Fiamma with the first model of a bag she created for her mother Wanda.

If Salvatore Ferragamo will go down in the history of fashion for his immense creativity in the design of shoes, Wanda Ferragamo will probably have an equally important place for her management of the business, which has made the brand famous all over the world, allowing the company to establish a network of over 500 sales outlets and expand its production from shoes to accessories, men's and women's wear, spectacles, perfumes and watches, but which above all has consolidated the reputation of Ferragamo, founding it on its tradition. And last but not least we have to thank Wanda and her children for having preserved the founder's creations for future generations, as testimony to an exceptional talent and, above all, to a strong culture of the product, based on the aesthetics of the everyday, on innovative and functional beauty. This is still the lynchpin on which the whole activity of the Ferragamo enterprise turns, from the training of its staff to its publicity.

In 1995, conscious of the value of this legacy, the Ferragamo family decided to present the history of the company to the public, and especially to younger people, always on the lookout for stimuli and points of reference. And so the Salvatore Ferragamo Museum was set up at the company's headquarters in Palazzo Spini Feroni, in demonstration of the fact that fashion has become part of the culture and art of a country.

Fiamma Ferragamo
in 1967.

菲安玛·菲拉格慕，
1967年。

斯蒂凡娅·瑞奇　萨尔瓦托勒·菲拉格慕：不朽的传奇

世间以非凡的个人天赋谱写传奇人生，其职业生涯和个人奋斗的故事有口皆碑，流芳百世的不乏其人，这向人们证明了一个道理：世事尽在人为。萨尔瓦托勒·菲拉格慕便是其中之一。

1898年，萨尔瓦托勒带着他无与伦比的制鞋天赋，出生于阿韦利诺省的博尼托镇，一座意大利南部　小镇。他在职业上的进步速度惊人。九岁时，他为妹妹的首度领受圣餐制作了第一双鞋，随后便跟着当地的一名鞋匠开始了学徒生涯。十一岁时，他拥有了一家自己的小鞋店，为镇上阔绰的乡绅太太们创作精美的鞋子。然而，在既得的成功面前，他并不甘于现状（正像在他后来的人生经历中多次发生过的那样），于是决定前往那不勒斯完成他的职业培训 – 那里的制鞋工艺当时已达到极其精湛的水平。

年仅十六岁时，萨尔瓦托勒就已经学到了在意大利所能学到的一切制鞋技艺，因此，对知识的渴求驱使他决定前往美国，追随在那里的哥哥们，其实那里的制鞋业比这里早了只不过几年的时间。

在纽约下飞机后，萨尔瓦托勒辗转奔赴波士顿，在那里的一家鞋厂找了一份工作。但是，那里的经历让他大失所望。美国制鞋业高效的生产给萨尔瓦托勒留下了深刻的印象，但其产品却远不能让他满意。他发现，批量生产的鞋子与美国平均制鞋水平相比，在质量上还过得去，但与远在意大利家乡任何一位好鞋匠制作的鞋子相比，其款式和造型均显得笨重和压抑。

鉴此，萨尔瓦托勒劝说哥哥们迁至电影业正在兴起的美国西海岸的圣巴巴拉，萨尔瓦托勒意识到，那里完全依赖手工制作的奢侈鞋履前景看好，而且这正是技艺精湛的意大利鞋匠所擅长的。于是，他在那里开了一家小店，为顾客修理和订制鞋履，晚上则在当地的大学进修足部解剖学课程，希望能制作出既美观优雅又舒适、实用的鞋履，这是他加入制鞋业之初便一直为之努力的目标。这几年的积累为他后来的发展，以及菲拉格慕尺码体系的创建奠定了坚实基础。这个以其名字命名的尺码体系，在其创立者于1960年去世之后，广泛应用于鞋品的批量生产中，成为品牌卓绝地位的标志。

美国电影公司向菲拉格慕下的第一份订单一委托他为一部西部牛仔电影制作靴子一为他带来了声名鹊起的机会。从那时起，菲拉格慕在无声电影的导演和明星中的声誉便与日俱增。

波拉·尼格丽（Pola Negri）、玛丽·碧克馥（Mary Pickford）和洛蒂（Lottie）姐妹、葛罗莉亚·史旺逊（Gloria　Swanson）以及梅·威斯特（Mae　West）等都是菲拉格慕的老主顾，即使在银幕以外，也都纷纷穿菲拉格慕制作的鞋品。菲拉格慕主要擅长制作女鞋，尽管确实设计过一些男士鞋款，并为许多电影以及如鲁道夫·瓦伦蒂诺（Rodolfo　Valentino）等好友制作过男鞋。当1923年美国电影业迁移到好莱坞时，菲拉格慕也随之一同前往，并在贝弗利山庄主要干道之一的好莱坞林荫大道Las　Palmas角开办了"好莱坞皮靴店"（Hollywood　Boot Shop）。塞西尔·戴米尔（Cecil　B.　De　Mille）、詹姆士·克鲁兹（James Cruze）、大卫·瓦克·格利菲思（David Wark Griffith）、拉乌尔·沃尔什（Raoul

Walsh）等导演委托菲拉格慕根据影片的服装图创作与之搭配的鞋品。女演员们竞相购买他的新奇鞋款，其中倾注了年轻的萨尔瓦托勒非凡的想象力和大胆尝试各种技巧与材质的热情，这与女鞋市场强烈的需求是分不开的。

然而，随着与美国第一批百货商店—纽约的萨克斯（Saks）百货公司以及旧金山的爱玛格耐（I. Magnin）公司的合作，大量订单纷至沓来，经常难以完成，因为在美国很难找到技术熟练、能够胜任手工制鞋的工匠。

1927年，为了寻找合格的鞋匠，萨尔瓦托勒决定重返意大利，并选择以优美艺术和精湛工艺而享誉全球的佛罗伦萨作为新的商业基地。

佛罗伦萨，这座孕育艺术家成长、创意和灵感以及无数杰作诞生的城市，为菲拉格慕提供了一方理想的天地，使他得以施展自己奇异非凡的创造力，缔造这座文艺复兴之城的当代神话。他意识到，高品质的手工产品辅以佛罗伦萨这座独一无二的城市的理念蕴含着强大而深远的寓意，能够使他的顾客，尤其外国顾客，觉得拥有一双菲拉格慕鞋品就好像获得了一件凝聚着佛罗伦萨艺术和文化传统的珍品一般。鉴此，菲拉格慕决定在佛罗伦萨成立他的第一家真正的公司—萨尔瓦托勒·菲拉格慕，从此他的名字便成了一个品牌的名字。

菲拉格慕凭借在海外积累的经验，在这片沃土上掀起了一波创新浪潮。他将美国制鞋业的生产工序运用到手工化生产中来，形成人工装配生产线，鞋匠成为了特定工序的专家。同时，他在生产中引入了美国尺码体系，经过他的调整，这一尺码系统不仅适应脚的不同长度，而且也适应脚的肥瘦。他发明了多项全新的技术方案，诸如用于承载足弓的钢质鞋底弓形垫等。多年以来，他发明了一系列引领时尚潮流的创新款型专利：从完全随意的发挥，到尝试各种材质，无论是极尽精致、奢华的材料，还是最前沿的创新材料，包括较为传统的材料类型，菲拉格慕都加以采用。这些鞋履完全是采用非同寻常的材料，通过大胆的颜色搭配和装饰制作而成的，例如用来制作草帽的稻草辫成了精致鞋款的鞋面，而产自Tavarnelle的花边得益于菲拉格慕的创意，也在鞋履上找到了新的应用领域。作为一个时代感极强的人，菲拉格慕始终追求当代艺术的推陈出新。为此，他聘请了当时意大利最具创新精神的未来派杰出艺术家卢奇奥·文那（Lucio Venna）为他策划首个广告促销活动以及在鞋品标签上印制的品牌标志。作为那个时代最杰出的工业设计师之一，他发明的款型均依照产品的功能要求设计相应的外观。他所创作的许多独特非凡、举世无双的杰作，以其无与伦比的精致华美和对细节极致的追求，犹如一件件艺术珍品。同时，他为自己每一项具有批量生产潜力的创意都申请了专利，直面工业化生产带来的挑战。前不久，据位于罗马的国家档案馆调查，菲拉格慕共拥有近四百项涵盖装饰、工艺改进、发明以及商业领域的专利，记录了这位艺术创作技巧大师在其整个职业生涯中卓绝无限的创造能力。

菲拉格慕于20年代末和30年代初所创作的鞋履，以精美绝伦的鞋面装饰和强烈、鲜明的色彩而独树一帜，尤其在面料与皮革的拼接作品中，他大胆运用各种极不寻常的色彩组合。而在别出心裁的鞋帮上，蜿蜒曲折的线条搭配以几何图案，其创作灵感来源于当时的抽象艺术。与此同时，菲拉格慕从佛罗伦萨多种多样的工艺传统中汲取丰富灵感，范围包括建筑装饰中的铸造到到当地金匠制作的精巧嵌花，并在其中以古典或东方艺术风格的图案加以交替运用。

菲拉格慕一方面潜心研究与众不同的装饰造型，以实现特定的装饰效果，另一方面，他极为注重鞋履良好的功能性。

然而，由于经营不善，加之1929年的美元大幅贬值以及随之而来的经济危机，迫使菲拉格慕不得不中止生产，并于1933年关闭了地处Mannelli街57号的首家工场。但是他并未气馁，又在位于佛罗伦萨中心Tornabuoni街区的费罗尼—斯皮尼大宅

Dress by Giovanna Ferragamo. Spring/Summer 1974.

Suit by Giovanna Ferragamo. Fall/Winter 1972.

Dress by Giovanna Ferragamo. Spring/Summer 1974.

乔瓦娜·菲拉格慕设计的女装，1974年春夏系列。

乔瓦娜·菲拉格慕设计的套装，1972年秋冬系列。

乔瓦娜·菲拉格慕设计的女装，1974年春夏系列。

Ferragamo's drawing
by Brunetta. 1987.

Ferragamo's suit. 1969.

布鲁奈塔（Brunetta）
创作的菲拉格慕素描，
1987年。

菲拉格慕套装，1969年。

Salvatore Ferragamo

（Palazzo Spini Feroni）新租了厂房，并以更大的精力和热情重新投入到制鞋以及向美国出口的贸易中，期间他谨慎经营，避免再犯之前的错误，并努力在本国和欧洲客户中树立声誉。他很快东山再起，并于1938年买下了费罗尼—斯皮尼大宅（Palazzo Spini Feroni），将第二层作为生产工场，第一层用作商店。同年，他又在伦敦老庞德街（Old Bond Street）和罗马Condotti街开办了两家分店。

在这些年中，菲拉格慕设计的每一款鞋履几乎都以精致的构造细节、和谐的对称性以及完美的重量和尺寸均衡比而著称，堪称艺术珍品。以软木制成的楔形鞋跟可谓那个时期菲拉格慕最为声名远扬的创新。菲拉格慕于1937年申请并获得了此项专利，然而起码在此两年以前，楔跟已经风靡全球时尚界，成为那个时代优雅品位的标志。楔形鞋跟的开发最初是为了满足一项功能性需求—提高鞋跟，并给予足弓稳定的支撑，并以巧妙和富有想象力的方式解决伴随埃塞俄比亚战争的爆发而出现的一大难题：意大利因受国际联盟的经济制裁，许多进口材料，其中包括菲拉格慕一直用于制作鞋底金属弓形垫的德国钢材受到影响。楔形鞋跟为诸如菲拉格慕等的艺术家提供了比鞋帮和鞋底更大的发挥其创造性想象力的表面空间。

经济制裁加剧了意大利国内物资匮乏与能源短缺问题，然而，却激发了菲拉格慕的发明创造才华，这不仅体现在装饰领域，更体现在技术的革新方面。菲拉格慕将葡萄酒瓶的软木塞串接在一起，外面包上皮革，从而设计出一款独特鞋跟；此外，他为一项皮革替代品的制作流程申请了专利。他还发明了透明的人造树脂鞋跟和拼接木质鞋底，其鞋帮采用酪朊塑料制成或者用玻璃装饰，仿效车轮或者缝线的卷轴。

菲拉格慕对于普通材料有着天生的青睐，他从三十年代初开始广泛使用纤维、稻草、羊毛线以及玻璃纸（一种糖果包装材料，可以形成闪亮、厚实而又起褶的表面）等各种面料，充分显示了奢华并非取决于所用材料的价值，而在于其中的创意和优良工艺。

Giaguaro silk crêpe
scarf. Fall/Winter
1986–87.

Fulvia Ferragamo with
her creations in 1971.

Fall/Winter Collection
1994–95.

"Giaguaro" 丝巾，
1986-1987年秋冬系列。

富尔维亚·菲拉格慕与她
的设计，1971年。

1994-1995年秋冬系列。

Men Fashion Shows:
Fall/Winter 2006–7 and
Spring/Summer 2007.

男装时装展，2006-2007
年秋冬系列与2007年春
夏系列。

即使在五十年代国际达显贵族开始对佛罗伦萨情有独钟之前，菲拉格慕就已与众多社会名流建立了良好的个人关系，包括尊贵的王后、贵族和女明星，她们纷纷亲临费罗尼—斯皮尼大宅（Palazzo Spini Feroni）布满壁画的贵宾室，让菲拉格慕为她们量脚制鞋，并聆听他有关穿着打扮的最新建议。

二战结束后边境重新开放以及贸易的恢复对于菲拉格慕以及整个意大利设计行业来说，都标志着一段黄金时期的开始，他们跃跃欲试准备大展鸿图，并期待着获得来自评论界以及国际市场的广泛赞誉。而萨尔瓦托勒·菲拉格慕则成为了时尚界意大利梦幻与格调的杰出代言人。1947年他设计了透明尼龙细线制成的鞋帮，并将其用于制作一款"隐形"凉鞋。正是凭借这款凉鞋，他在达拉斯荣获了有着"时尚界奥斯卡"之称的尼曼·马库斯（Neiman Marcus）设计奖，共同分享该奖的还有服装设计大师克里司汀·迪奥（Christian Dior）。

50年代后期，菲拉格慕开始思考公司的未来，以及如何应对日益激烈的竞争形势和国际市场严苛的需求。

在不到十年的时间里，意大利的工业发展达到了前所未有的水平，其增长速度高于欧洲其他任何国家。与美国建立政治联盟为意大利带来了经济合作伙伴，这在实践中已转化为向欧洲销售美国机械、工业设备以及专利技术。工业化的蔓延导致消费品逐步平民化，而意大利的劳动力成本相比其他欧洲国家仍保持在较低水平，这样就得以保持价格稳定，同时令意大利产品在国际市场越来越具有竞争力。

意大利的经济转型、国际市场上新的鞋履制造商及品牌的不断涌现以及意大利国内市场需求的增长，促使萨尔瓦托勒·菲拉格慕不得不重新考虑公司的生产策略。1948年，他曾拒绝了一家美国工厂以每年5万美元，在长达20年的期限内有偿在其生产的一个机制鞋品系列中使用"Ferragamo Debs"品牌的提案。但十年后，他被迫做出妥协，以保持菲拉格慕鞋履的市场地位并增加收入。在保持部分鞋品继续手工制作的同时，菲拉格慕设计了几个价格相对便宜的二线品牌，并冠以"Ferragamo Debs"和"Ferrina Shoes"商标。这两款鞋品在英国生产，其中60%采用手工制作，其余40%由机器生产。与此同时，他开始丰富产品系列，创造出第一款皮包以及饰有以意大利主要城市及其艺术珍宝为灵感而设计的图案的印花丝巾，并于1959年将自己的名字冠于二女儿乔瓦娜为Lord & Taylor百货公司设计的运动服装系列。

1960年萨尔瓦托勒·菲拉格慕溘然长逝，公司经营的重任落到了他的遗孀蔓达以及六个儿女肩上，她们各自在公司担任起职责分明的职务。

在此后十年里，萨尔瓦托勒·菲拉格慕成为了一家由女士经营的公司。此前一直仅仅扮演妻子与母亲双重角色的蔓达，投身带领公司克服种种困难，从一家注重狭窄市场的小型公司转型为一家产品远销三十五个国家和地区的大型企业。乔瓦娜继续开发女式成衣系列，扩大产品品种，从而赢得了自1965年起全面参加在佛罗伦萨著名的Pitti宫举行的意大利时装展的资格。

菲拉格慕的大女儿菲安玛，作为六位儿女中唯一一位曾与父亲并肩工作过的第二代家族成员，肩负起鞋履领域的创意指导重任。她做出重要决策，引导公司从手工制作转向工业化生产，在制造流程中仅保留少量手工工序。假如公司要扩大销量并实现更具竞争力的价格，同时又保持奢侈品的特点，那么这种转移就必不可少。"我喜欢钻研艺术、文学和音乐，"菲安玛叙述道，"而我也不打算放弃这些追求。但我的父亲坚信我的未来就在公司。最终他说服了我。一开始，我试图在工作与学习两者之间保持平衡，但工作日渐让我更加痴迷，直到最后我选择了工作。我曾经对制鞋一无所知，但父亲总是站在我身边鼓励我，教我如何选材，如何了解工艺品质，如何找到迎合当前时尚潮流的款式。父亲是一位非常严格的老师，

Men *Oxford* shoe
hand stitching phase.

男士牛津鞋手工缝制工序。

Prototype. The *Gancino*
shape. Women watch
with stainless steel case
and diamonds. 2008.

原型表款。"Gancino"造
型女士腕表，不锈钢表壳，
嵌饰以钻石。2008年。

Black satin sandal
with a *Gancino* diamond
ornament. 2001.

黑色绸缎凉鞋，饰
有"Gancino"钻石，
2001年。

同时又考虑周到，善解人意。这不仅是对我，对他手下的制鞋工匠也同样如此。假如有人犯错，父亲总是能找到方法先表扬他的功绩，然后指出他的错误。"

父亲去世时，菲安玛不得不面对最初这一品牌随着萨尔瓦托勒的过世而失去市场信任的严峻形势。1961年1月，菲安玛奔赴伦敦展示她的首个系列鞋履，令她极为吃惊的是买家对其作品的反响不仅十分积极，甚至是狂热。"他们问我，"菲安玛继续说道，"这些设计中是否有我父亲的作品。我告诉他们，我们拥有许多由我父亲设计但未投入生产的鞋款，其数量之多足以让我们维持好多年。这一回答让他们树立了信心，所以订单纷至沓来。我达到了自己期望的结果—赢得他们的信心并确保传统得以延续。"每一季度，被媒体誉为"年轻时尚大师"的菲安玛和乔瓦娜两姐妹，都会在意大利、英国伦敦以及美国推出新的产品系列，这些都是菲拉格慕曾于五十年代设立公司，在北美地区经销菲拉格慕产品地方。姐妹俩上午和下午向买家展示她们设计的款式，而晚上则到女修道院过夜，因为她们的母亲蔓达女士认为两个年轻女孩留宿旅馆显然是不妥的。

二十世纪50年代的经济腾飞对60年代产生了真实可见的影响，工业进步突飞猛进，各行各业繁荣昌盛。即使是最高档产品的细分市场，如奢侈品市场，也明显提高了自己的份额。市场的注意力，从五十年代仍是主要参考对象的精英消费

者，转向了地位稍低的中产阶级；后者往往希望通过使用独一无二的产品，并借助品牌的形象彰显自己的社会名望，比如汽车或皮鞋。事实上，这段时期恰好见证了设计师的名字与标志作为产品品质保证与社会声誉的重要元素的建立，这一切的发生并非偶然。对于菲拉格慕公司而言，这种潮流的直接影响就是决定改变品牌标志。"Ferragamo's Creations"这一品牌名称，作为菲拉格慕鞋品的标签，一直沿用到五十年代，此后便替换为公司缔造者萨尔瓦托勒·菲拉格慕的书写体签名，用于标识各种产品、专卖店、包装及广告材料，以保持萨尔瓦托勒·菲拉格慕的创新形象旺盛的生命力。

制造商们对于市场的新趋势做出了两种不同的反应。其中一些选择降低产品质量，以适应大规模生产，而像菲拉格慕公司等的其他一些制造商，则出于维护传统与至尊品牌的需要，决定拉开中档产品与自己赖以成名的高品质产品之间的差距，将产品打造为独一无二的杰出作品并将销售重点集中到一些精选客户上。菲拉格慕公司一方面继续依靠品牌闻名于世的精湛技艺和对完美品质的极尽追求，制造高档时尚产品和量脚订制的鞋履，将每一种款式的产品制作为几乎绝无仅有的艺术珍品，成为时尚的标志；另一方面，菲拉格慕公司在成衣系列的基础上，开发出批量生产的产品系列，并将注重细节、材质等品牌顶级产品线所具有的特点融入其中。历经十余年的发展变化，量脚订制鞋履的产量逐渐下降，公司开始将注意力集中在更加广泛的国际分销业务及产品的多样化方面，例如，公司从1965年起开始批量生产包品系列。

萨尔瓦托勒公司一直极为重视鞋履的舒适性与合脚性，同时并重优雅美观，为维护这一标准，公司倾注了大量的心血。与此同时，公司的内部结构在短时间内经历了重要调整。五十年代，公司以手工方式，凭借其内部的750名工匠每天可制作350双鞋，到60年代，菲拉格慕公司通过那不勒斯地区以及佛罗伦萨附近工业区的一些专为其加工产品的小型工厂，将日产量提高至2000双。但是制鞋流程的创意部分以及决定鞋品合脚程度的鞋模原型和鞋楦的制作工序，仍保留在公司内部完成。1964年萨尔瓦托勒的长子费鲁齐奥加入公司担任管理职务；70年代费鲁齐奥的妹妹富尔维娅紧随其后加入公司，负责丝绸配饰、丝巾、领带以及礼品的设计与生产；而费鲁齐奥的弟弟莱昂纳多则挑头建立了菲拉格慕男装部，生产男式服装与配件，随后又负责公司在远东地区的业务拓展工作。最后加入公司的家族成员是他们最年幼的弟弟马西莫，承担了经营美国市场的重任，这一市场一直都是菲拉格慕公司最为关注，同时也是利润最为丰厚的国际市场。

蔓达和她的儿女们在巩固和延伸品牌根本原则的同时，找到了将秉承萨尔瓦托勒留给他们的不断创新传统发扬光大的最佳方法。曾以无数鞋款和创意掀起制鞋业深刻变革的伟大设计师已经离去，鉴此，公司注重走大都会风格之路，将设计与皮革品质和精致做工完美融合，保持了菲拉格慕注重细节与材料创新的一贯传统。如果说菲拉格慕公司的产品在萨尔瓦托勒时期植根于他的原创款式、不断创新以及间或的异想天开，那么自他过世以后，则建立在一种精心设计的优雅风格的基础上，以便满足更为广阔的市场需求，迎合不同的服饰文化。

这一发展思路并不意味着在公司在创新和试验方面已停滞不前。从防滑鞋底到碳纤维公文包，在公司众多的专利当中，最值得一提的是为菲安玛赢得鞋履创意尼曼·马库斯（Neiman Marcus）大奖的螺旋高跟和雕花高跟，此为在继父亲赢得这一奖项的二十年之后她再次获此殊荣；更为重要的还有今日菲拉格慕公司最负盛名的两款标志："Vara"和"Gancino"标志。前者是一款饰有蝴蝶结的无带鞋品的标志，自于1978年创作以来，未曾有过任何大的改动，至今仍保持良好的销量。而后者则是，从一幅50年代的已模糊不清的照片判断，一种绊扣装饰，最早是在萨尔瓦托勒·菲拉格慕设计一款包品时使用的，然而使这一标志在全球闻名遐迩的无疑是菲安玛和她为母亲蔓达所设计的首款皮包。

如果说萨尔瓦托勒·菲拉格慕因其在鞋履设计中无与伦比的创造力而在时尚界英名高筑的话，那么蔓达·菲拉格慕则可以以自己在公司管理上的成就而分享这一殊荣。正是在她的管理下，菲拉格慕公司成为了享誉全球的品牌，建立起拥有逾500个销售网点的全球性网络，并将产品从鞋品拓展到配件、男式和女士时装、太阳镜、香水以及手表等领域，最为重要的是进一步极大巩固了菲拉格慕的声誉，使品牌传统得以延续和发展。最后但同样重要的是，蔓达和她的儿女们保护了品牌创始人为后世留下的的杰出创作，这些作品是菲拉格慕先生旷世才华的证明，更彰显着以日常生活美学、创新的功能美感为基础的产品中所蕴含的文化底蕴。此外，这仍是菲拉格慕公司从员工培训到广告宣传等各项活动的核心。

1995年，意识到菲拉格慕留下的鞋款的巨大价值，菲拉格慕家族于是决定向公众，尤其是年轻人，展示公司的发展历史，从而对他们有所激励，成为他们参照的目标。鉴此，公司在位于费罗尼 – 斯皮尼大宅（Palazzo Spini Feroni）的总部建立了萨尔瓦托勒·菲拉格慕博物馆，以向世人展示时尚已成为一个国家文化和艺术不可分割的一部分这样的事实。

F by Ferragamo
perfume. 2006.

"F"标志菲拉格慕香水，
2006年。

Cristina Morozzi   A Contemporary Myth

Nouvelles mythologies was recently published, fifty years after *Mythologies* by Roland Barthes. The latter, which came out in 1957, was the first systematic portrait of the consumer society seen through its misrepresentations, symbols, icons and myths. The new publication, written by several authors and edited by Jérôme Garcin – who supports Barthes' semiological and occasionally sarcastic principles – gives examples of what are considered myths in the new millennium.

Ferragamo is worthy of being cited in the book; it has all the characteristics of a myth, if, as is claimed by the anthropologist Marc Augé, "myth is a story whose foundations cannot be questioned". The archival collection comprising more than 13,000 pieces held in the Florentine museum of Palazzo Spini Feroni, the company's historic main offices, is an unquestionable basis for what to all intents and purposes can be said to be "a myth".

In 2008 the Ferragamo company will celebrate its eighty years. This is a record, considering that Emilio Pucci's company (daughter Laudomia is currently image director and vice-president) was sixty in 2007 and that Christian Dior, the company that in 2007 celebrated one hundred years since its foundation, has been a "maison" for only sixty years. Moreover, Ferragamo remains entirely in family hands, while other resurrected designer labels are drawn to luxury, investment banking or new ownership groups, convinced that the acquisition of an archive is enough to keep alive a label's prestige. In the history of the Italian manufacturing industry, Ferragamo is therefore one of the most long-lived names and, on account of its distinguishing qualities, lends itself well to representing the best of "Made in Italy", which is nearly always the history of "families" sustained by perseverance (sometimes bordering on obstinacy) and visionary flair.

The eightieth birthday, and that the company remains a family concern, are enough to make Ferragamo a myth. More importantly however, Ferragamo has all the attributes to be a contemporary myth. It is not only the weight of years, or a history studded with records and patents, that makes it a myth. Rather, it is the company's absolute modernity; the fact that, in important ways, it has always been in tune with the boldest and most inventive trends in contemporary creativity. In retracing the company's history, no dust from the past or aura of nostalgia is found, only an ability to be continuously in harmony with the design methodologies of new generation designers. Ferragamo's eighty years – always in concord with contemporary creativity – demonstrate how vision and imagination are timeless, and hence an expression of a productive and eternal present, and how faith in creative excellence knows no failure.

These remarkable affinities are not so much formal – given that forms, though subject to sudden revivals, also suffer time – as much as affinities relating to aptitude and process. To account for some of them, it is worthwhile looking at some aspects of Salvatore's life history. He was the cobbler of Bonito who at a tender age became "shoemaker to the stars" of Hollywood.

I don't intend to digress on episodes that have the ring of an epic, all documented

Pietro Annigoni, *Portrait of Salvatore Ferragamo*, oil on canvas, 1949.

皮耶特罗·埃尼格尼
（Pietro Annigoni）画，
《萨尔瓦托勒·菲拉格
慕肖像》，布面油画，
1949年。

Apparatus for supporting injured limbs. Patented January 1924.

受伤下肢支撑器。
1924年1月获得专利。

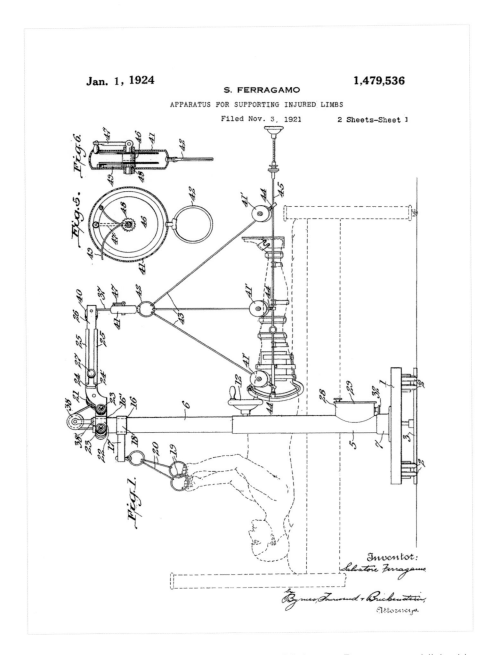

in *Shoemaker of Dreams. The Autobiography of Salvatore Ferragamo*, published in London in 1957 by George G. Harrap & Co. and which is "unputdownable", like an adventure book. But I do want to examine Salvatore's methodological convictions and coherent and instinctive flair, typical of a designer; I want to look at his faith in the founding principles of the project: the form that springs from, and is enhanced by, the technical and ergonomic answer to function. Salvatore learnt his trade by apprenticeship in Bonito and travelled to America as an emigrant to join his brothers; it is not by accident that as soon as he had acquired some familiarity with the language he enrolled in night courses in human anatomy at the University of Southern California. He was a shoemaker and feet interested him. His obsession was "the relentless search for the secret, which for centuries had escaped the shoemakers of the entire world: the secret of shoes that always fit well". On this "obsession", and on his innate talent and thirst for knowledge, he built a legend.

I think it is worthwhile highlighting his strong will to be an artisan, to patiently and skilfully create by hand at a time when machines were being introduced that were eliminating hard work. It is also worthwhile examining his steadfast conviction that what counted in his footwear was quality and excellence, and that these resulted not only from materials and design, but also working with precision, taking time and checking every detail.

"I went to the factory", he recalls, "and everything I knew how to do, the machines could do in the blink of an eye. But I wasn't impressed; I was horrified. That wasn't being a shoemaker; it was hell... I was a shoemaker, not a finisher, a cutter, or a hemmer; I didn't feel like doing any of those fragmentary jobs for those mass-produced shoes. In that context, individual skill didn't matter at all". This declaration expresses a clear and resolute defence of his craft and pride in creative virtuosity. In a modern and post-modern world this attitude would sound retrograde and shortsighted, but today, in an age the anthropologists call "hyper-modern", it is totally contemporary. Principally in the area of furniture design, there is a new generation of designers dedicated to artisanship, and this continues to grow.

It was thought that as a result of the industrial age, and then the computer age, hands had been laid to rest. Everything could be machine-made, even what at one time was the prerogative of expert artisans.

On the contrary, as though to contrast Rapid Prototyping – a method for creating complex, interconnected and embellished 3D models automatically through a plotter connected to a computer – artisan work is enjoying a new vogue in the third millennium. Designers themselves are becoming artisans. In their study-laboratories, they dedicate themselves to manual work, and in the process rediscover traditional tools: not as dilettantes, like the English Bloomsbury group at the beginning of the twentieth century (whose members included Virginia Woolf and Vanessa Bell), but as true and tireless professionals, committed to an almost maniacal perfectionism, exercised in the creation of increasingly complex works in traditional materials such as wood, porcelain, marble, plaster and fabric. What is hand-made gives added value to the design too, which is born to be standard and machine-made. In relation to production time, the worker is no longer unavoidably slavish to it, because the project becomes a magnificent obsession. The more time spent on it, the more valued is the work. In contrast to the rotational moulding used to create a polypropylene armchair in thirty minutes, there are young designers who take pride in having dedicated months – working

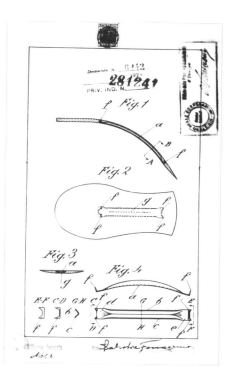

Support device for the shoe sole arch, the so-called waist. Patented January 1931.

Ferragamo shoes were renowned for their lightness. Two comparable shoes are on the scales: 130 grams are needed to make the Ferragamo shoe balance with the other.

鞋底拱形（又称鞋腰）支撑装置。1931年1月获得专利。

菲拉格慕鞋履一向以轻盈闻名。天秤两边分别放上用作比较的两款鞋履：菲拉格慕鞋履比其他鞋履轻130克。

eight hours a day – to create a one-off piece. The time taken to create something manually enhances personal skill, and this becomes as legitimate as the idea.

Limitations give rise to opportunities. This has always been claimed as regards design and the principle continues to be valid even today, when all limitations appear easily surmountable thanks to technological progress. Harvey Molotch, professor of sociology at New York University and author of numerous essays on design, claims that "necessity stimulates innovation and in order to create it is necessary to fall in love with things". According to Molotch, the creativity crisis that appears looming on the horizon is due to the fact that, weighed down by the overabundance of goods, we are on the verge of feeling repulsed by the excess.

Salvatore loved feet: "I like feet", he wrote. "They speak to me. The moment I take them into my hands I feel their power, weakness, vitality and defects." With regards to materials he said this: "A shoemaker can decorate his models using an endless variety of materials. I have used diamonds and pearls (real and fake), gold and silver dust, precious hides… I have used satin and silk, lace and embroidery, crystals and mirrors, and the feathers and hide of ostrich, antelope, kangaroo, leopard, lizard, python and water snake. I have used fish skin, felt and transparent paper, snail shell and raffia, seaweed and wool… I have used beads, sequins, nylon (which is stronger than leather, notwithstanding its apparent fragility) and string covered in transparent paper."

The loss of prime materials, due to policies on sanctions imposed by the League of Nations in 1936, did not discourage Salvatore; on the contrary, it inspired him, forcing him to improvise. Two of his most successful ideas came from these very improvisations, from a box of chocolates and a piece of Sardinian cork. Attracted by the chocolates' transparent paper he thought of using it – together with coloured thread that shimmered through the paper – to make shoe uppers.

Towards the end of 1936 high-quality steel also disappeared, for the Ethiopian war effort. Salvatore had used steel to model a light and flexible lamina as the arch support, which was incorporated into the sole of every shoe. This strategy had made his shoes light – 130 grams in contrast to the 250 grams of other shoes – and durable. How could he maintain lightness and durability, the prized qualities of his shoes? He thought of filling the space between the heel and forefoot with light material and he began pressing and pasting together pieces of Sardinian cork. The first orthopaedic shoes were born. "In a matter of weeks", he records in his autobiography, "my wedge shoes became my most popular model. There was not a single woman who did not praise their comfort and that comfort was all in the cork. Rubber, in fact, would have made walking too springy. Cork, on the other hand, gave the impression of walking on cushions." Interest in raw materials was not, however, dictated solely by the need to find substitutes for increasingly scarce precious materials. It sprang from the enthusiasm of an artisan to experiment and challenge the imagination, and also from intellectual curiosity fed on what was happening in contemporary avant-garde circles.

On returning to Italy in 1927 he was certainly influenced by the Futurist movement proclaiming "the use of one hundred new materials". In the Manifesto of Futurist female fashion published in 1924 the Futurists wrote: "We will throw open the doors of fashion ateliers to paper, cardboard, glass, foil, aluminium, majolica, caoutchouc, rubber, fish skin, packing cloth, tow, hemp, fresh plants and living animals". Salvatore threw open the doors to cork, cellulose, nylon, raffia… Nor were the practices

Salvatore Ferragamo with his shoemakers. 1955.

萨尔瓦托勒·菲拉格慕和他的鞋匠们，1955年。

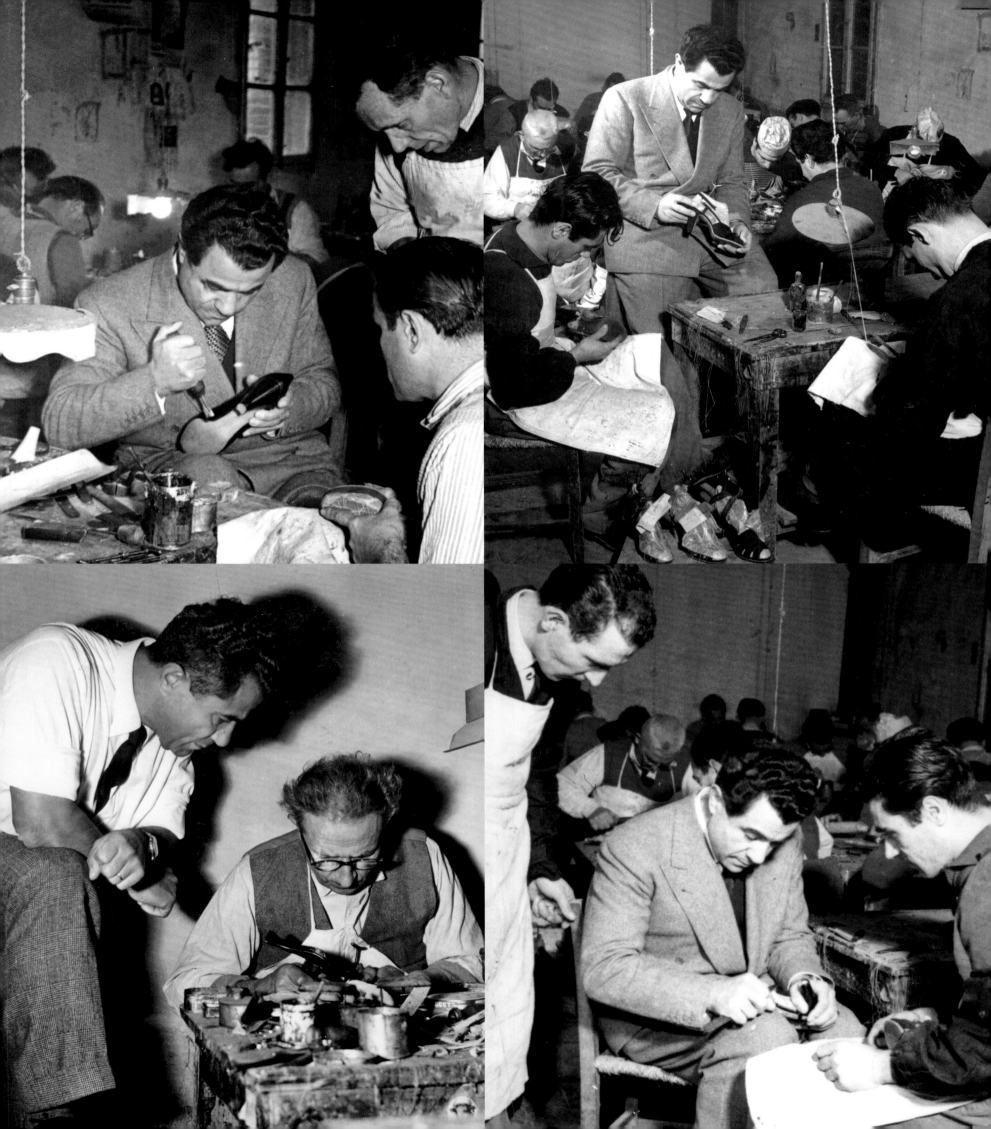

Straw upper of a
Salvatore Ferragamo
shoe. 1932.

Sonia Delaunay, *Without
title* (detail), gouache
on paper, 20 x 16.5 cm.
1930. Paris, Librairie
des Arts Décoratifs.

萨尔瓦托勒·菲拉格慕的
稻草鞋帮鞋品，1932年。

索尼娅·德兰奈（Sonia
Delaunay）画，《无
题》（细节），1930年，
纸面树胶水彩画，
20x16.5 cm。
巴黎，艺术装饰馆。

of Elsa Schiaparelli foreign to him. Close to the Surrealists and friend of Salvador Dalí and Jean Cocteau, Elsa incorporated metaphors from the Surrealist world into her clothes, using cellophane, rayon and synthetic rodophane, alternative materials with which even Salvatore was familiar. Ferragamo's 1938 rhinoceros-horn pointed shoes, his multicoloured wedge heel sandals created for Judy Garland, also from that year, and his 1939 shoes with satin uppers and sculptured cork wedge covered in kid, are all examples that reveal a strong association with Surrealist figuration.

A fervid creator, through instinct he was on the same wavelength as the designers and artists of the time. In 1947, when he was travelling on the Queen Elisabeth to receive the Neiman Marcus Award, he met Christian Dior (he did not even know his name) for the first time and realised that his shoes and Dior's clothes seemed to have been designed hand in hand. "It seemed strange", he wrote, "both Dior and I had made totally new models, and yet they coincided to such an extent that on the catwalk my shoes perfectly matched his clothes. But perhaps", he concludes, "it's not strange, because I feel that the direction of fashion is not the special prerogative of a single creator, but is in the air, as a kind expression of what the world desires."

It is in the air, but you have to know how to capture it, and perhaps sometimes predict it, by running ahead of prevailing taste. Salvatore had prophetic abilities and he knew it, confessing that he often anticipated fashion: "Many times", he wrote, "I was successful by standing out from prevailing fashion with models that were immediately popular. First it was with the French-style toe and later with the ortho-

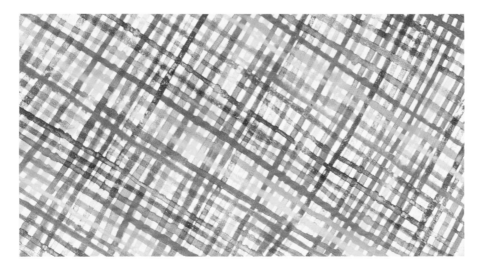

Raffia upper of a
Salvatore Ferragamo
shoe. 1942.

Sonia Delaunay, *Without
title, no. 1412* (detail),
gouache on paper,
9.5 x 27 cm. 1928.
Paris, Librairie des Arts
Décoratifs.

萨尔瓦托勒·菲拉格慕的
酒椰鞋帮鞋品，1942年。

索尼娅·德兰奈（Sonia
Delaunay）画，《无
题》，编号：1412，
1928年，纸面树胶水彩
画，9.5x27cm。
巴黎，艺术装饰馆。

paedic heel." As Andrea Branzi wrote in the special edition of *L'Europeo* magazine
published to mark the opening of the Museo del Design at the Triennale of Milan
(December 2007), Ferragamo's career path shows that in Italy "innovations are born
more from theoretical guesswork than from market necessity". The excellence of
"Made in Italy" does not spring from a system, but from visionary and intuitive creative people who are curious about the world and able to make the best use of the
wide terrain of artisan skills to give shape to personal risk. Italian creativity is an-
archical and difficult to bridle. It is for this reason that it always succeeds in aston-
ishing. For Salvatore the search for replacement materials was not dictated solely
by the needs of war. It was essentially his passion putting creativity to the test by
using non-conventional materials; it was a kind of obsession towards "impossible"
creations, like the invisible sandals from 1947, for which he won the Neiman Marcus
Award. The invisible sandals idea came to him via an employee who was passionate
about fishing and who, with a new type of nylon line, had caught a large fish in the
Arno. "The fish don't see it, he explained to me. And so I had found the material I
needed to create an idea of mine: shoe uppers that can't be seen."

His eagerness to explore non-conventional and preferably primary materials, transforming and renewing them to improve his skills in creating something of value, is
paralleled in the work of certain contemporary designers: for example, in Fernando
and Humberto Campana, the Brazilian brothers who created for Edra the sculpture
chairs with battens used to build the favelas in São Paulo; in Leonor Ippolito, the

Ferragamo sandals
created for the Neiman
Marcus event. 1947.

菲拉格慕凉鞋，Neiman
Marcus奖项获奖作品，
1947年。

young Portuguese designer, who created high-quality necklaces and earrings with chocolate wrapping paper; in Stuart Haygarth of London, who assembles thousands of lenses from glasses, or plastic remains found on the beach, to create striking chandeliers; and in the Belgian Charles Kaisin who transforms old pieces of furniture by covering them in a thick coat of newspaper. Salvatore's skill in interpreting the nature of materials draws him close to Gaetano Pesce, the artist/designer and creator of well-known masterpieces, who has revitalised design aesthetics, thrilling the DNA of the materials, mainly the artificial ones.

What is being done today in fashion and design can be found in Ferragamo's archives: spotted zebraed shoes, Roman-style sandals, embroidered shoe uppers, gold and silver wedges, etc. Mosaics are back in fashion, not only to cover walls, but also as a shimmering, many-sided surface for art objects. The "Bisazza" outsized silver-plated mosaic sculptures, created by Studio Job, the Dutch artistic duo known for their gothic-style visions, caused a sensation at the 2007 Milan Furniture Show. The non-conventional use of mosaic material is striking, as it enriches

Favela wooden chair
by Fernando and
Humberto Campana.
Edra Production. 2003.

Sandal in bark. 1930.

"Favela" 木椅。费尔南
多（Fernando）和汉别
多 · 堪帕纳（Humberto
Campana）共同设
计，Edra 公司制作，
2003年。

树皮材料凉鞋，1930年。

the gigantic shapes of domestic furnishings, reproduced with calligraphic accuracy. Salvatore had made use of mosaic as far back as 1936 in the form of gilded, mirrored tesserae to cover the cork heels of sandals with Roman-style fastening and a toe-cap formed by two bands of black satin and kid. This anti-conventional use of materials gave heels the sparkle of jewels. And what of needlepoint, created only in white and known as "Tavarnelle" lace, once used exclusively to embellish clothes, underwear and linen?

At the end of the 1920s, when Salvatore returned from the United States and settled in Florence, he began to use it for shoe uppers, with the added novelty of colour. Floral and geometric arabesques lent the shoes a unique play of "now I see you, now I don't", transforming the upper into a kind of foot tattoo.

Today lace is back in vogue. The designer Brunella Caccaviello, for example, used "Cantù" lace in her *Flos ad Florem* collection to create extra-fine earrings and brooches in the French couture jewel tradition. Embroidery is also making a comeback, which Salvatore began to use, mainly in the form of the chain stitch, from the mid-1930s. Embroidery, which was thought confined to keepsake albums, is being used increasingly by designers to decorate furniture and furnishings. Sofas are being embroidered in smock stitch, as Patricia Urquiola did for Moroso; lampshades are being made in tapestry stitch and cushions in cross stitch with designs taken from web graphics; and even ceramic vases are being embroidered, as has been done by Hella Jongerius, the Dutch designer and champion of artisan tradition aesthetic values. If we short-circuit time, it is obvious – above all if we consider the most recent figurative trends – how staggeringly modern is Salvatore Ferragamo. He is more modern today than yesterday, when purism and minimalism were pointing towards austerity and essentiality in created things.

In his passionate autobiography there are annotations on research into forms and materials, and reflection on creating and embellishing, which are the bread and butter of young designers, who are becoming increasingly similar to Renaissance workshop artists, willing to get their hands dirty to create works that have the feel of unique, one-off pieces.

Salvatore Ferragamo died in 1960 at the age of 62, leaving six children and a very young but courageous wife, Wanda, who today remains at the company's helm. He also left a heritage of patents, shoe models, documents, photographs and work

tools. He had built a legend by constantly experimenting new forms and materials and working with his hands. How could this legend be kept alive? How could a heritage built on passion, or it must be said, the obsession for a craft, be managed? First of all, by focusing on the technique of producing models that guarantee comfort and lightness, the main qualities of Ferragamo footwear. But for the name to prosper, it was not enough to continue making shoes well. Ferragamo was a shoe shop and the shoemaker had died. It was therefore necessary to transform Ferragamo into a brand that could survive life's misadventures and give it an international identification beyond the shoe product. Wanda understood that to do so it was necessary to abandon mono-production, move away from the limited sphere of accessories and expand into the production of other items. To become a designer label Ferragamo had to become more complete and move into clothing.

Elder daughter Fiamma, who had just turned twenty and had already worked alongside her father, was given the task of looking after shoes and bags. Giovanna, the second born, was to start a line of clothing.

Salvatore had never placed limits on his imagination and experiments. He was, as a creator, unbridled. Wisely though, the family chose a more moderate way: genius cannot be replicated. They preferred to concentrate on ergonomics, lightness and comfort to keep alive "the secret of shoes that always fit well". Knowing that Ferragamo's fortune, as claimed by Salvatore in his autobiography, was founded on "understanding the comfort of the hundreds of thousands of people for whom I made shoes, and not on design, models or workmanship. We used and use revolutionary forms that give the arch support, enabling the foot to move about like a pendulum in reverse, leaving it free". The Queen of Romania, the wife of King Carol and mother of King Michael, had this to say when she tried on her first pair of Ferragamo shoes: "with these shoes my toes feel like they are swimming. This is a freedom they will never take away from me!" And to "make the toes swim" clients come from all over the world, today as much as yesterday.

Saying the family chose the moderate way does not mean they abandoned elegance and creativity. In fact Ferragamo prestige is living and evolving on the very bino-

Tide chandelier by Stuart Haygarth. 2005.

Hairy chair by Charles Kaisin. 2005.

"潮汐"装饰灯，斯图亚特·哈葛斯（Stuart Haygarth）设计，2005年。

"绒毛"椅子，查尔斯·凯辛（Charles Kaisin）设计，2005年。

Mon Cheri Ferrero
earrings by Leonor
Ippolito, 2005.

Sandal in cellophane
and silk. 1957.

"费列罗蒙雪丽"耳坠，
利昂·利普里图
（Leonor Ippolito）设
计，2005年。

玻璃纸和丝绸双面料凉
鞋，1957年。

mial elegance/comfort, enlivened by a good dose of fantasy, which is in the family
and is nourished by models from the archives. It seems contradictory to speak of
archives, of what was and what remains, with reference to the fashion world, which
is dynamic and ephemeral by nature and burns new ideas every season. In fashion,
as in all other sectors, the new is built on the sediments of the past. The best fruit
comes from soil that has had diverse sowing cycles; so too with companies, the new
must be nourished from what belongs to history. Experimentation, trials, successes
and even mistakes line the difficult road that from a project leads to a product. The
archive of what has been produced fertilises the ground for the new to grow. The
Ferragamo family has had a special "fertiliser". They have grasped its potential;
they have preserved and enhanced it, by searching the world for Salvatore's models. And they have built a museum, open to the public, in the Palazzo Spini Feroni
in Florence. It is a living museum, not only because it nourishes the company, but
more so because it includes exemplars that, in terms of inventiveness, are timeless. They do not refer to the past but to today (or even tomorrow); they express, in
a striking way, what is being created and produced today. Those who are inspired
by Ferragamo – and in the fashion world there are many – know his works are not
revivalist but avant-garde. True inventions are timeless: in design above all, this is
proven by the success of certain pieces that have been in production for more than
thirty years, and by the increasing number of revivals of past pieces. Salvatore,
a true designer, was gifted with an approach that corresponded in many ways to
that of new-generation designers, above all Dutch. In his autobiography he stated:
"Among the many models that come to mind I select, in general, those that are in
tune with fashion's current direction, but sometimes also certain models that antici-
pate the times, because a creator must be allowed to create; he mustn't suppress
his ideas simply because the world is not yet ready to receive them."
Even Marcel Wanders or Tord Boontje, the new generation of Dutch creative artists
(promoters of a fairy-tale-like design based on the intensive use of decoration) and
who are already considered stars, do not view fashion with suspicion; rather, they
are inspired by it to give glamour to their creations. But at the same time, they pro-

voke and predict by using the latest technology such as laser cutting or hardening resins. They are precursors, having launched a decorative trend into the puritan design world at a time when minimalism was insisting on the reduction of forms to their bare bones. Like Salvatore in his time, the most interesting designers of today work in a hybrid way, combining artisan work with high technology to achieve surprising effects from every kind of material, be it noble or poor.

Post Salvatore there are no creative fireworks, only prudent selection and management of proposals. To give identifiability and strength to the brand it was necessary to create symbols, something that lasts in time. This can be said of the Omega symbol for example. The same can be said of the *Vara* shoe created in 1978. Born from an error, a flat bow rather than a full one, and in a rainbow of colours, the shoe became, thanks to its unending success, one of the best examples of the brand. Similarly, the case of the Post it by 3M sprang from experiments that gave life to a sticker so weak it could not be used; and the Scott Towels, which came to life when the machine producing toilet paper created a batch with the wrong thickness. These great success stories sprang from mistakes.

In the 1970s Fulvia put foulards into production which became very characteristic. Grasping their media value, Salvatore already had had a number created by well-known illustrators, favouring symbols relating to "Italianness". Among the many exuberant patterns, which to some extent evoke Salvatore's febrile creativity, those relating to the animal world were precursory: stylised ornamental plants, tropical flowers and spotted animals in bold patchwork. The 1980s saw the appearance of foulard garments, distinguished by bold figurative over-abundance. In recent times there are also examples that appear to derive from the founder's creative daring: bags woven with wooden beads, the tricot ones in straw and cord, which refer back to Salvatore's experiments with replacement materials; and finally last season's bags in wood, which are part of the current trend towards a return to natural, sculptural, carved, inlaid and even lathe-worked forms.

If one retraces Ferragamo's 1980s, there are many examples of correlation between his work and the history of design; the connections between Salvatore's approach and that of new-generation artists is startling. Today these connections are being renewed, thanks to the family's ability to use the archival heritage, and not by replicating in a banal way, but by drawing from that heritage Salvatore's unique and visionary spirit. The revival of certain historic models, which seem totally contemporary in shop-front windows, is further evidence of parallels with what is happening in the design sector. Many well-known furniture companies are reproducing certain debut pieces, for example, the *Bambole* series of upholstered pieces by Mario Bellini (B&B production), or the *Fiocco* armchair by Busnelli, both from the 1970s but absolutely contemporary. Ferragamo revivals – since 2007 they have a special space in certain flagship stores and from the isolated episode are becoming common policy – are to be understood not as a sign of creative crisis but as an awareness of the timelessness of certain designs. To be "in fashion" it is not enough to be inspired by an archive; it is necessary to know how to distil its values, the values that speak of permanence.

Even a hurried acknowledgement of the heritage of these first eighty years reveals that there are many examples of what is "permanent", enough to nourish directions yet to be designed.

克莉丝提娜·莫瑞兹　当代神话

继罗兰·巴特（Roland Barthes）的著作《神话学》（Mythologies）出版50年后，《新的神话》（Nouvelles mythologies）一书也于不久前出版问世。前者著于1957年，是首部通过剖析社会中的传说、象征、偶像及神话而对消费社会进行系统刻画的著作。而这部由多名作家联手执笔，并由崇尚巴特的符号学、间或支持讽刺主义的耶罗姆·加尔辛（Jérôme Garcin）统编的新版图书，列举了许多新千年中被奉为神话的范例。

菲拉格慕，正是值得载入该书的经典；如果按照人类学家马克·奥盖（Marc Augé）所申述的：“神话是指起源无从考证的传奇故事。”那么，菲拉格慕承载着神话所应具备的全部特征。在费罗尼—斯皮尼大宅（Palazzo Spini Feroni），公司历史悠久的办公总部中的博物馆内，逾一万三千双珍贵鞋款的珍藏见证了菲拉格慕无论从任何意义上讲均可被称作“神话”的无可辩驳的基奠。

2008年，菲拉格慕公司将迎来80周年庆典。相比艾米利奥·彪奇（Emilio Pucci）的公司（目前其女Laudomia担任公司的形象总监和副总裁）于2007年迎来了60周年庆典，而克里司汀·迪奥（Christian Dior）公司于2007年虽号称百年历史，但称得上“名门”的时间也不过只有区区60年，这的确创造了一项纪录。此外，鉴于其他许多复兴的设计品牌纷纷依托于名门贵族、投资银行或新兴的控股集团，而菲拉格慕公司仍完全掌握在自己的家族手中，因为他们深信如此庞大的馆藏足以使品牌赫赫声誉始终保持勃勃生机。因此，在意大利制造业的历史中，菲拉格慕公司可谓是最悠久的企业之一，其无与伦比的卓越品质已成为“意大利制造”的最佳典范，一直以来秉承传统（时而在固守精髓的基础上加以拓展）和天马行空的才华而不断延续其“家族”发展史。

公司的80周年华诞，以及公司仍处于家族的管理之下这一事实，足以使菲拉格慕成为神话。然而更重要的是，菲拉格慕还具备成为当代神话的所有属性。不仅岁月的沉淀，或沉积着光辉成就和专利的历史充满了传奇；更确切地说，公司非凡卓绝的现代意识—即菲拉格慕在前沿创意方面与最为大胆创新的时尚潮流始终保持和谐一致的事实—才是真正的神话。追溯公司发展历程，我们丝毫看不到过往的尘埃或怀旧风格，而唯有与新一代设计师不断取得协调统一的设计理念。菲拉格慕公司的八十载岁月，始终与前沿创意齐头并进，演绎出设计理念和创意何以经久不衰并进而成为内涵丰富的永恒形象的最佳诠释，同时展现出菲拉格慕品牌对于卓越创意的不懈追求。

这些奇特的相似之处并非十分中规中矩—鉴于家族企业尽管出现过短暂的复兴，但其形式也已受到时间的淘汰—并不像与个人禀赋和制造工艺相关的相似点那样明显。为说明其中一些相似点，我们有必要深入了解萨尔瓦托勒生活经历的某些方面，这位来自博尼托的鞋匠，年纪轻轻时便成为了好莱坞“明星御用之鞋匠”。

我并不打算因这一英雄史诗般的故事离题万里，所有传奇都在George G. Harrap & Co公司于1957年在伦敦出版的萨尔瓦托勒的自传《梦鞋匠》（Il calzolaio dei sogni）中有所记载，就像一部探险记那样令人爱不释手。但我的确希望探究萨尔瓦托勒作为设计师所特有的制鞋工艺理念及其始终如一的天生禀赋；我希望考察他对制鞋业的根本原则为何如此忠贞不渝：鞋品的造型源于利用技术以及人体工程学满足功能的需求，并因此而得到发展。萨尔瓦托勒在博尼托做学徒时掌握了这门手艺，尔后远渡重洋，移民美国，投奔他的哥哥们；当他渐渐熟悉英语后，又有意识地迅速在南加州大学注册，参加夜校学习人体解剖学知识。他是一名鞋匠，他对人类的双脚有着浓厚的兴趣。他痴迷于"对制鞋诀窍永不停息的探究，即脚与鞋和谐统一的诀窍，多个世纪以来，这一点已经在全世界的鞋匠身上消失殆尽"。正是依靠这种"痴迷"以及他与生俱来的天赋和对知识的渴求，萨尔瓦托勒缔造了自己的传奇。

我认为值得着重指出的一点是他对于成为一名工匠的强烈愿望，以自己的耐心与技术用双手打造出一双又一双的鞋品，尽管当时制鞋行业引入的机械设备消除了这项耗时费力的工作。同样值得考证的是他对于鞋品卓越品质的不变信念，这些信念不仅来自材料与设计，同时源于精致做工、所花的时间和对每个细节的考究。

他回忆说："我走进工厂里去，我会做的一切工作，机器都能在眨眼之间完成，但我没有为之赞叹，反而觉得毛骨惊然。做鞋可不是这个样子的，这是个地狱。我是个鞋匠，不是个修边工人，我做的并非是替大量生产的鞋子修理零碎工作。这里面没有工艺可言，丁点儿也没有。"这些宣言表明他对于捍卫手艺的明确而坚定的立场以及对于创新能力的自豪。在现代社会乃至后现代社会，这种态度显得思想倒退且目光短浅，但如今，在这个人类学家称为"超现代社会"的时代，这完全是一种现代思想。尤其是在家具设计行业中，就出现了新的一代设计师，专注于自身的手艺，而且呈现出有增无减的趋势。

人们曾经认为，由于工业时代以及之后的计算机时代的到来，手工技艺可以功成身退了。机器可以制造出任何产品，甚至那些曾一度只有能工巧匠才能制作的产品。事实恰恰相反，手工作品好像故意和快速原型制作技术作对一样，在新千年迎来了新一轮的流行，后者是一种通过与计算机相连的绘图器创作出互联而又精心修饰的复杂3D模型的方法。

设计师自己正在演变为工匠。他们在研究室中，全心投入各种手工制作，并在这一过程中重新发掘各种传统工具：这倒不是想成为20世纪初英国的布卢姆斯波里（Bloomsbury）文化圈（成员包括维吉尼亚·伍尔夫（Virginia Woolf）以及瓦内萨·贝尔（Vanessa Bell））那样的半吊子专家，而是不懈追求的真正专业工匠，追求一种近乎疯狂的完美主义，并将其付诸实践：使用木材、陶瓷、大理石、石膏以及织物等传统材料创作愈发复杂的作品。手工技艺还可提高设计的附加值，尽管这样的设计原本可以使用机器进行标准化生产。从制造时间方面看，工人不再毫无选择地沦为它的奴隶，因为整个过程已经变成为一项高度痴迷的工作。花的时间越多，作品的价值就越高。与30分钟即可制造出聚丙烯扶椅的滚塑技术不同，许多年轻设计师更加为耗费数月时间（每天工作8小时）专心致志地制作一件作品而感到自豪。手工创作一件作品所耗费的时间可以磨练个人技能，而这就像创意一样公平合理。

局限性创造机遇，长期以来这一直与设计联系在一起。这一准则同样适用于今天，尽管技术进步可让所有局限性看起来都可以轻松地得到解决。纽约大学的社会学教授以及众多设计著作的作者哈维·莫罗托（Harvey Molotch）宣称"需求激励创新，要创造，就需要对各种事物情有独钟"。他认为，日渐逼近的创新危机乃是因为商品过度充裕带来的重压，这令我们正处在对其产生排斥感的边缘。

萨尔瓦托勒对脚情有独钟。他写道："我喜欢脚，脚会跟我说话。我只稍用手触摸，便可感受到脚的强处和弱点、生气或颓败。"在谈及制鞋材料时，他说："美无极限，设计无止境。鞋匠能采用无穷无尽的物料来装饰自己的设

Novus, Spring/Summer 1940.

"Novus"，1940年春夏系列。

Cork wedge heel
covered by silver mirrors.
1939.

软木楔根，覆盖银色镜
面，1939年。

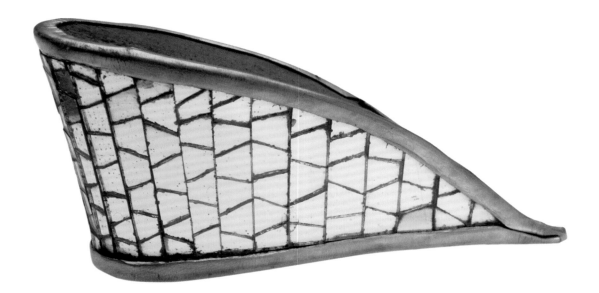

计，我用过钻石和珍珠，有天然的也有人造的；用过金沙和银沙；用过珍贵的皮革……我使用过缎子和丝绸、蕾丝和刺绣、水晶和镜片；用过鸵鸟、羚羊、袋鼠、豹、晰蝎、巨蟒、水蛇的翎毛和皮革。用过鱼皮、毡布、透明纸、蜗牛壳、酒椰、海草和羊毛……还用过珠子、小金属片、尼龙（别看它外表脆软，其实比皮革还要强韧），甚至是透明"纸线"，也就是包着线的透明纸。"

由于国际联盟从1936年起对意大利采取制裁政策，制鞋的主要原料出现短缺，但这并没让萨尔瓦托勒灰心丧气；恰恰相反，这反而激发出他的灵感，迫使他即兴发挥。他的最成功的两项创意即来自这些特别的即兴创作：其一源自一盒巧克力，而其二则源于一枚撒丁岛软木塞。受巧克力透明包装纸的吸引，他突发奇想地使用这种材料—以及贯穿于透明纸中间闪闪发亮的彩色丝线—制作鞋帮。

到1936年年底，优质钢材因为埃塞俄比亚战争也已失去供应。萨尔瓦托勒原本使用钢材制造一种轻盈而富有弹性的薄片作为嵌入每双鞋鞋底中的脚拱支架。这种方法可以使鞋子变轻—与其他鞋子相比，其他鞋子重为250克，而他制作的鞋子仅有130克—同时经久耐穿。

怎样才能保持轻盈与耐久—菲拉格慕鞋品的这些广受褒奖的品质？他想到了在鞋跟与前脚掌的空隙中填充轻质材料，然后便开始将撒丁岛软木塞压实并粘接在一起。于是第一双带有矫正功能的鞋品诞生了。萨尔瓦托勒在自传中写到："几个星期内，楔跟鞋已成为我最受欢迎的一款设计。穿上楔跟鞋的女性，都向我大赞鞋子穿得舒服。这种舒适的感觉其实来自软木。换了是橡胶的话，走起路来会有一种急躁的反弹力；软木给双脚的感觉，却像踏在软垫上般舒服。"然而，萨尔瓦托勒对于原材料的浓厚兴趣，并不仅仅体现在寻找替代品，以替代日渐稀缺的珍稀材料上。这实际上源于一名工匠对于试验以及挑战自身想象力的渴望，同时也源于他对当时前卫时尚领域发生的事件的求知欲。

1927年返回意大利后，菲格拉慕不可避免地受到未来派运动及其宣扬的"采用100种全新材料"的影响。在1924年发表的未来派女性时尚《宣言》中，未来派主义者写道："时尚设计室的大门将向全新的材料敞开，包括纸张、纸板、玻璃、箔纸、铝、陶器、弹性橡皮、橡胶、鱼皮、包装布料、粗纤维、大麻、新鲜植物以及活体动物等。"萨尔瓦托勒则向软木、纤维素、尼龙和酒椰纤维等材料敞开大门；同时，他对埃尔莎·夏帕瑞丽（Elsa Schiaparelli）的创作实践也毫不陌生；这位法国时装设计师与多位超现实主义艺术家关系密切，是萨尔瓦托勒·达利（Salvador Dalí）、吉恩·科克托（Jean Cocteau）的好友，将超现实学派理念融入自己的服装设计，尝试使用玻璃纸、人造纤维和若丹膜等萨尔瓦托勒亦非常熟悉的独特材料。萨尔瓦托勒于1938年设计的犀牛角尖头鞋、于1938年为茱蒂·嘉兰（Judy Garland）设计的彩色楔跟凉鞋以及1939年设计的绸缎鞋帮和外包小山羊皮的软木雕花楔跟鞋品，都体现了菲拉格慕与超现实主义表现手法之间的深厚联系。

作为一名热忱的创作者，菲拉格慕凭借本能与同时代的设计师和艺术家保持着不谋而合的默契。1947年，当菲拉格慕搭乘伊丽莎白女皇号前去领取尼曼·马库斯（Neiman Marcus）大奖时，他与克里司汀·迪奥（Christian Dior）首次相遇，那时他甚至没听说过迪奥的名字，却惊讶地发现自己设计的鞋款与迪奥的服装仿佛联袂设计一般。"这似乎有点离奇。"他写道，"我和迪奥设计的都是全新款式—但它们竟是如此的相衬，我的鞋和他的服装穿在模特儿身上，搭配得简直堪称是天衣无缝。"他总结道："这不足为怪。许多年来我一直深信，时尚潮流并非某个设计师的专美，而是'捉摸不定'的—甚至可以说，那是世界愿望的一种显现。尽管捉摸不定，但你必须知道如何捕捉它，有时或许需要领先于流行品位，预见它的走向。萨尔瓦托勒便拥有这种预知能力，他了解这一点，承认经常能够预测即将流行的时尚。他写道："我往往因而领风气之先，有好几次甚至成功突破当前的时尚潮流，让我的新设计马上风行起来—最初是我的法式鞋头，然后有楔形鞋跟。"正如安德尔·布莱兹（Andrea Branzi）在为庆贺三年展设计博物馆开放而出版的《欧洲》专刊（2007年12月）中所说，菲拉格慕的职业生涯显示，在意大利，"创新设计，比起市场需求，更多地来源于理论推测"。"意大利制造"的卓越品质并非出自某个体系，而是源自拥有远见卓识和与生俱来的创新

Studio Job for "Bisazza".
2007.

Studio Job为Bisazza公
司设计的产品，2007年。

意识的人们，他们对这个世界充满好奇并能够充分利用工艺技术所带来的巨大张力，勇敢地将个人创意付诸现实。意大利人的创造力横溢不羁，难以驾驭。正因如此，它总能够成功地推出令人惊叹的杰作。对萨尔瓦托勒而言，寻找替代材料不仅仅是因为战争导致了短缺。实质上，这更是出自他热衷于将创造力应用于非传统材料的试验探索；这是一种对"不可能"创作的迷恋，这一点在他于1947年创作的隐形凉鞋上得到了验证，该鞋款品为他赢得了尼曼·马库斯（Neiman Marcus）设计大奖。隐形凉鞋的想法来自于一名热衷钓鱼的员工，他用一种新的尼龙鱼丝在亚诺河钓到了一条大鱼。"鱼儿看不见鱼丝，"他告诉我说，"由此，我找到了实现隐形鞋面的创意所需要的材料。"

菲拉格慕热衷于开发非传统的和更为普通的制鞋材料，并将它们改进、创新以提高制作更具价值鞋品的技艺。他在此方面取得的成就可与当时一些前卫的设计师媲美：例如，费尔南多（Fernando）和汉别多·堪帕纳（Humberto Campana），这对巴西兄弟为Edra公司设计创作的雕塑座椅，采用了建造圣保罗市的贫民区Favela所用的木板条。年轻的葡萄牙设计师，利昂·利普里图（Leonor Ippolito）使用巧克力包装纸制作出品质优雅的项链和耳坠。伦敦设计师斯图亚特·哈葛斯（Stuart   Haygarth）汇集数以千计的眼镜镜片和丢弃在海滩上的塑料垃圾，创作出令人惊叹的装饰灯具；还有比利时的查尔斯·凯辛（Charles Kaisin）在旧家具外覆盖一层厚厚的报纸而对家具进行改造。萨尔瓦托勒对材料质地恰当演绎的技巧拉近了他与艺术设计师吉唐诺·佩茨（Gaetano Pesce）之间的距离，后者创作了许多举世闻名的杰作，并且极大地丰富了主流人造材料，令设计美学再次兴盛。

当今时尚和设计界的流行元素在菲拉格慕的作品中可见一斑：带斑马条纹的鞋品、罗马风格的凉鞋、刺绣鞋帮、金色和银色的楔跟等等。马赛克又重返潮流，不仅应用在墙面装饰上，而且也用于营造艺术作品闪烁和多面的表面效果。荷兰艺术家组合Studio   Job以其哥特式风格的设计而闻名，他们为Bisazza公司创作的超大型镀银马赛克雕塑在2007年米兰家具展览会上引起了轰然大波。马赛克材料的非传统应用能够带来摄人心魄的效果，它在精美绘画的烘托下丰富了室内家具的大型款式。早在1936年，萨尔瓦托勒就开始在创作中运用马赛克。他使用镀金的马赛克嵌片覆盖凉鞋的软木鞋跟，并搭配罗马风格绊扣，鞋头以两条黑色缎带与小牛皮带构成。这种反传统的材料应用赋予鞋底如珠宝般熠熠闪烁的光芒。

那么，针绣花边又是如何应用在制鞋中的呢？这种被称为Tavarnelle蕾丝的材料通常只有白色，其应用仅局限在服装、内衣和床上用品的装饰上。上世纪20年代末，萨尔瓦托勒离开美国返回佛罗伦萨定居后，开始将针绣花边用于制作鞋帮，并赋予新颖的颜色。花卉和几何形状的蔓藤图饰给鞋品带来若隐若现的效果，令鞋帮犹如绘在脚面的花纹一般。

如今蕾丝已经重返时尚。例如，设计师布鲁内拉·卡卡维略（Brunella Caccaviello）在她的Flos ad Florem系列中便采用Cantù蕾丝，在法国时尚珠宝传统风格的基础上，制作出极尽精美的耳坠和胸针。刺绣同样再次流行。萨尔瓦托勒从30年代中期开始，便将其主要应用到链形缝制法中。曾一度认为只会出现在纪念相册上的刺绣，现在已越来越多地被设计师们应用于家居装饰。例如，派翠西娅·乌尔乔拉（Patricia Urquiola）为Moroso家具公司设计的沙发，就饰有打缆针法的刺绣花纹；还有以织锦刺绣制作的灯罩和十字针法刺绣的坐垫，设计灵感来源于网状图案；刺绣甚至还应用在陶瓷花瓶的装饰中，正如荷兰设计师、传统美学观念的拥护者，赫拉·洪格利乌斯（Hella Jongerius）在其作品中所做的各种尝试。如果我们缩短时间轴，纵观最近的装饰潮流—便可清晰地看出，萨尔瓦托勒·菲拉格慕的设计如此富有现代气息。当创新设计中的纯粹主义和极简主义日益倾向质朴与真髓风格时，菲拉格慕的设计一天比一天更富有现代的元素。

在菲拉格慕的自传中，记载着他对制鞋工艺和材料所做研究的评注，以及对创作和装饰的领悟。这些是年轻设计师们的饭碗，他们已经越来越像文艺复兴时期，在工作室中埋头创作的艺术家，不辞劳苦地创作出独一无二、绝无仅有的作品。

萨尔瓦托勒·菲拉格慕于1960年逝世，享年62岁，留下6个儿女和非常年轻、勇敢的妻子蔓达，此后至今，蔓达始终肩负着公司经营管理的重任。另外，菲拉格

慕还留下了大量专利、鞋品模型、文献、照片和制鞋工具等宝贵遗产。他凭借自己的双手，不断尝试全新的工艺形式和制作材料，缔造了传奇的人生。然而，如何保持这一传奇生生不息呢？如何管理这笔建立在热情，或者说对制鞋工艺无限痴迷上的遗产呢？首先，要将重点放在带来舒适、轻巧穿着效果的制鞋工艺上，此为菲拉格慕鞋品的主要特质。但是，为了使菲拉格慕公司更加驰名，仅凭不断生产优质鞋品是远远不够的。菲拉格慕公司是一家鞋店，然而如今鞋匠已经与世长辞。因此，必须将菲拉格慕转变为一种品牌，这样才能在逆境中求得生存，并在全球树立起不仅仅包括鞋品的认知度。蔓达明白，要做到这一点，则必须放弃单一的生产模式，从狭窄的配件领域着手寻求产品的多样化。为打造时尚设计品牌，菲拉格慕公司则必须走综合经营之路，向服装业迈进。

刚满20岁时就追随父亲一起工作的长女菲安玛，肩负起公司鞋品和箱包产品的运作重担。二女儿乔瓦娜则负责开发时装系列。

萨尔瓦托勒从不为自己的想象力和大胆尝试设定限度，作为一个创作者，他可谓天马行空。而他的家族则明智地选择了更为中肯的发展之路：毕竟天才无法复制。他们更注重于提高鞋品的工效学特性以及轻巧、舒适性，以此永葆"鞋品合脚的秘诀"。众所周知，菲拉格慕公司的财富，正如萨尔瓦托勒在自传中描述的那样，是建立在"悉心了解千百万顾客的舒适需求，而非设计、款式或工艺"的基础上的。这始终依赖于"一种具革命性的鞋楦；这鞋楦通过支撑脚拱，令脚的作用变得像一个倒转了的钟摆，放任其舒适自在。"罗马尼亚皇后，即卡洛尔二世国王的妻子、迈克尔国王的母亲，在第一次穿上菲拉格慕的鞋子时说道："穿了这双鞋子，我的脚趾就像在游泳一样。这种自由自在的感觉，他们怎样也无法从我身上夺去。"今日，乐于"让脚趾游泳"的顾客仍从全球各地涌来，高涨的热情丝毫不减。

我们说菲拉格慕家族采取中肯策略，并不意味着他们摒弃高雅与创新。事实上，菲拉格慕公司的声誉正在高雅与舒适这两大特性的基础上不断延续和发展，这是其家族接手后完善管理和菲拉格慕博物馆珍藏鞋模孕育的结果。就充满活力和昙花一现时尚潮流天性，季季都推出新创意的时尚领域来说，谈论已成历史的产品，哪些已经消逝，哪些依然流行，似乎完全自相矛盾。在时尚界，如同在其他行业一样，新产品是以历史积淀为基础的。最卓著的成果来自经历多轮回发展周期的历史沉淀，企业也不例外，新的产品必然是从以往的旧产品孕育而来。从设计构思到新产品的发布必须经历一段由实验、尝试、成功，甚至失败铺成的艰难历程。已成为历史的产品是孕育新产品成长的土壤的肥料。而菲拉格慕家族则拥有这样的特效"肥料"。他们已经掌握其巨大的"肥力"；通过在世界范围内为萨尔瓦托勒的鞋模寻找市场，他们使其得到了发扬光大。他们现已在佛罗伦萨费罗尼—斯皮尼大宅（Palazzo Spini Feroni）中建造了一座向公共开放的博物馆。这是一座"栩栩如生"的博物馆，不仅因为它是公司发展的营养来源，更因为它拥有众多就创新意义而言永恒不朽的典范作品。他们不甘于过去的辉煌，而更注重当前，甚至未来的发展；他们以引人注目的方式展示今天不断创作和生产的作品。那些追随菲拉格慕设计风格人一在时尚界不胜枚举一深悉菲拉格慕的作品并非旨在复兴，而是要引领潮流。真正的创新必然永世长存：尤其在设计领域，已经连续生产三十多年的某些成功作品以及越来越多历史作品的复兴，便是有力的证明。萨尔瓦托勒，作为一名名副其实的设计大师，其设计理念上的天赋在许多方面都与新一代设计师不谋而合，尤其是荷兰设计师。他在自传里写道："最初会有多项设计浮现在我的脑海里。然而，我通常会从中选出明显能与当前时尚相衬的那几个款式；但有时候，我也会选择一些较前卫的设计—因为创作者必须拥有创作空间，不能仅仅因为世界还没有准备好，就把新的理念完全扼杀。"

Hand crocheted *Marisa* tote with wooden details. Spring/Summer 2007.

手工钩织的"Marisa"手提包，带有木质装饰。2007年春夏系列。

Sandal in silver
kid, chosen for the
Ferragamo's Creations
in 2007 and originally
created by Salvatore
Ferragamo for Evita
Perón in 1947.

银色小山羊皮凉鞋，入选
2007年"菲拉格慕创意系
列"，原创于1947年，
由萨尔瓦托勒·菲拉格慕
为艾维塔·贝隆（Evita
Perón）设计制作。

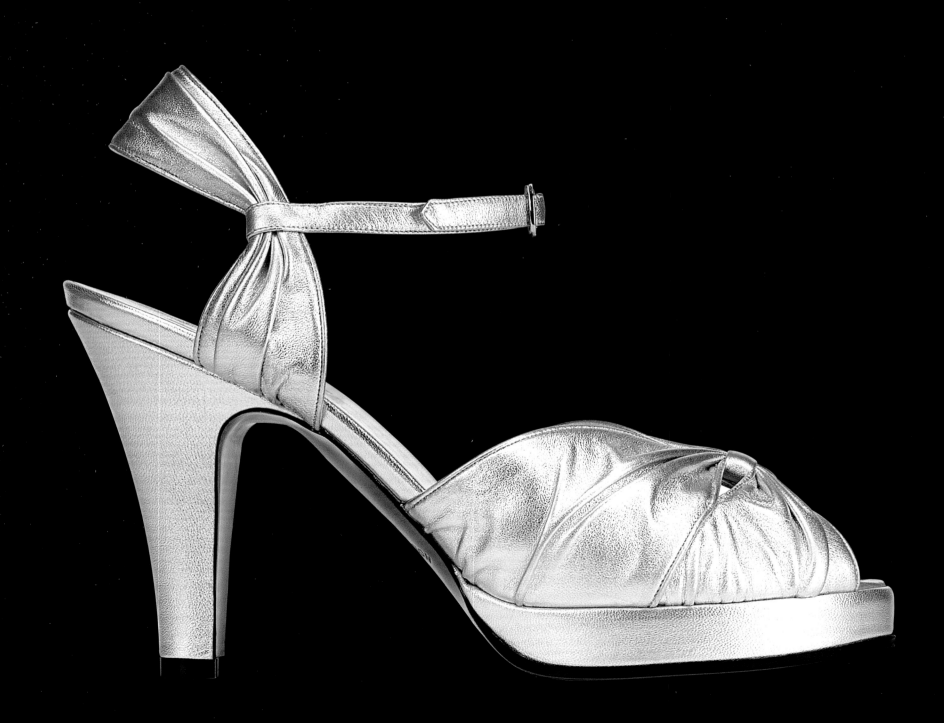

即使马塞尔·旺德斯（Marcel Wanders）或托尔德·布恩杰（Tord Boontje）这样的新生代荷兰创新艺术家（提倡大量采用饰物的童话式设计风格的代表人物）以及那些早已功成名就的设计师，对时尚也同样毫不怀疑，相反，他们深受时尚启发而为其作品增光添彩。但与此同时，他们运用激光切割和树脂硬化等最新技术，掀起和推动新的时尚浪潮。他们作为先驱，在清教徒式的设计王国激起了一股装饰潮流，令一度为极简主义所占据的设计领域焕发出勃勃生机，前者坚持简化主义形式以回归作品本来面目。就像那个时代的萨尔瓦托勒，如今最新奇的设计师以一种兼容并蓄的方式进行创作，将手工作品与高新技术加以结合，尝试各种各样的材料，达到令人惊艳的效果。

萨尔瓦托勒后时代，再没出现过如烟花般轰动一时的大作，取而代之的是谨慎的抉择与方案管理。公司意识到，为提高品牌的知名度和竞争力，必须设计独特的标志，以在漫漫的时间长河中历久弥坚。"Gancino"标志就是一个极好的例子。诞生于1978年的Vara女鞋也是如此。该款女鞋诞生于一个小小的失误，原设计中皮革蝴蝶结被罗缎蝴蝶结取代，配饰彩虹般缤纷的色彩，最终成为长盛不衰的畅销女鞋，是品牌中最经典的事例之一。类似地，3M公司报事贴（Post-it）的诞生，源于黏着力太小而不能使用的胶带；同样，Scott牌纸巾则源于用机器生产卫生纸时，弄错了一批产品的厚度。这些取得巨大成功的产品都源于偶然的失误。

20世纪70年代，弗尔维亚推出柔软丝绸产品的量产，逐渐发展成特色鲜明的产品品牌。意识到媒介的巨大价值后，萨尔瓦托勒曾邀请许多知名画家绘制体现意大利风情的画作。这些丰富华美的图案，在某种程度上激发了萨尔瓦托勒澎湃的创造力。动物王国相关主题的图案最受推崇：风格独特的装饰植物、热带花卉以及带有斑纹的动物，这均采用大胆的拼接工艺制作而成。20世纪80年代见证了丝绸服饰的兴盛，它们以大胆醒目、极为饱满的装饰图案独树一帜。近年来，还呈现出许多在萨尔瓦托勒大胆新颖作品的基础上的翻新之作：用木珠编织的手提包、采用稻草和绳索罗纹针织的手提包，其渊源可追溯到萨尔瓦托勒尝试使用各种替代材料所作的创作；以及最近一季的木质包品，是当下回归自然、雕刻、镂花、镶嵌甚至车工等装饰潮流的极佳演绎。

回睦20世纪80年代，我们可以发现菲拉格慕公司的许多作品都与设计发展历史息息相关；萨尔瓦托勒与新生代艺术家们在创作方式上的不谋而合令人惊叹。如今，随着家族充分利用馆藏瑰宝，从中汲取萨尔瓦托勒非凡独特、奇异烂漫的设计灵感一而绝非平庸地复制，品牌与前沿潮流的联系也在不断发展的同时而被赋予了新的内涵。一些经典款式的复古鞋品，在商店的橱窗中彰显着非凡的当代气息，进一步见证了菲拉格慕与设计领域中时刻涌动的时尚潮流的默契一致。许多知名家具公司也纷纷再次创作一些他们创建伊始时的设计，例如B&B公司的设计师马里奥·贝利尼（Mario Bellini）设计的装饰家具"Bambole"系列，以及布思尼利（Busnelli）的"Fiocco"座椅，两者均创作于70年代却依然焕发着鲜明的当代气息。从2007年开始，一些旗舰店将菲拉格慕复古系列从其他产品中独立出来，摆放在特殊位置，并渐渐成为菲拉格慕公司普遍的陈设原则。这些复古产品应当看作是对菲拉格慕不朽设计的意识觉醒，而绝非创意危机的征兆。为紧跟时尚脚步，仅仅依靠以往设计提供的灵感显然不够，因此知道如何从中汲取代表着至高品质的价值尤为必要。

即使对菲拉格慕公司首个八十年的历程所凝聚的丰富传统加以仓促的肯定，仍揭示出许多不朽的作品，足以为今后的设计指明方向。

"If I could maintain my output only by using the methods of mass production, and if the only way I could maintain my standards and my reputation was the manufacture of hand-made shoes, why not a system of making hand-made shoes by mass production?" (from *Shoemaker of Dreams. The Autobiography of Salvatore Ferragamo*)

"如果维持产量的唯一办法就是大量生产，而维持我的标准和名声的唯一方法就是手制鞋，那何不借助大量生产的方式制作手制鞋？"（摘自萨尔瓦托勒·菲拉格慕的自传《梦鞋匠》）

Craftsmanship ── 工芸

"Throughout Italy, in both cities and poor villages, you can see cobblers sitting in their little shops surrounded by piles of shoes, bending over their lasts, under the light of a naked light bulb." Thus wrote Salvatore Ferragamo in his autobiography, describing the labour situation in Italy at the beginning of the twentieth century. In southern Italy in particular, footwear was made mostly by hand; standards, in terms of craftsmanship, were extremely high. When Salvatore emigrated to the United States, where the footwear industry was exploding, he decided to remain faithful to the Italian tradition, even though he developed that tradition with certain techniques learnt from industry. Back in Italy and established in Florence, Ferragamo widened the scope of his craftsmanship to uppers made with lacework, embroidery or straw, or with heels spattered with stones or lined with gold or silver, all the fruit of local expertise that was prized worldwide for its excellence, for the product quality of "Made in Italy".

When production diversified beyond footwear and became industrial to meet the needs of a changing market, the Ferragamo brand continued to draw on its heritage and preserved certain artisan aspects of its manufacturing. Focus on detail and passionate commitment to the craft of shoemaking were the keys to the brand's success.

"在整个意大利，无论是城镇还是贫困的乡村，随处可见鞋匠们坐在堆满了鞋子的小店里，借助着光秃秃的灯泡发出的光线，伏在鞋楦上工作着。"萨尔瓦托勒·菲拉格慕在他的自传中谈及20世纪初意大利劳动力状况时如此写道。尤其在意大利南部，鞋履大部分以手工制作完成，其工艺水准已达到极高的水平。当萨尔瓦托勒移民到制鞋工业繁荣发展的美国时，他仍决定奉守意大利的制鞋传统，甚至还借鉴了一些在该行业中所学的技术将这一传统进一步发扬光大。回到意大利并在佛罗伦萨建立公司后，菲拉格慕进一步拓展了制鞋工艺，如采用花边、刺绣或草编制作鞋帮，或者在鞋跟上缀饰宝石或镶嵌金边、银边。这些运用意大利本土杰出工艺制成的鞋履，以卓越的品质享誉世界，成就了"意大利制造"的品质保障。

随着产品品种的多样化进程而不仅仅局限于鞋类制品，以及为了满足不断变化的市场需求，生产过程不断向工业化发展，但同时菲拉格慕品牌始终坚持自己的传统，并继续保持其制作的艺术风格。精益求精和对制鞋工艺的执著追求是菲拉格慕品牌获得非凡成功的关键。

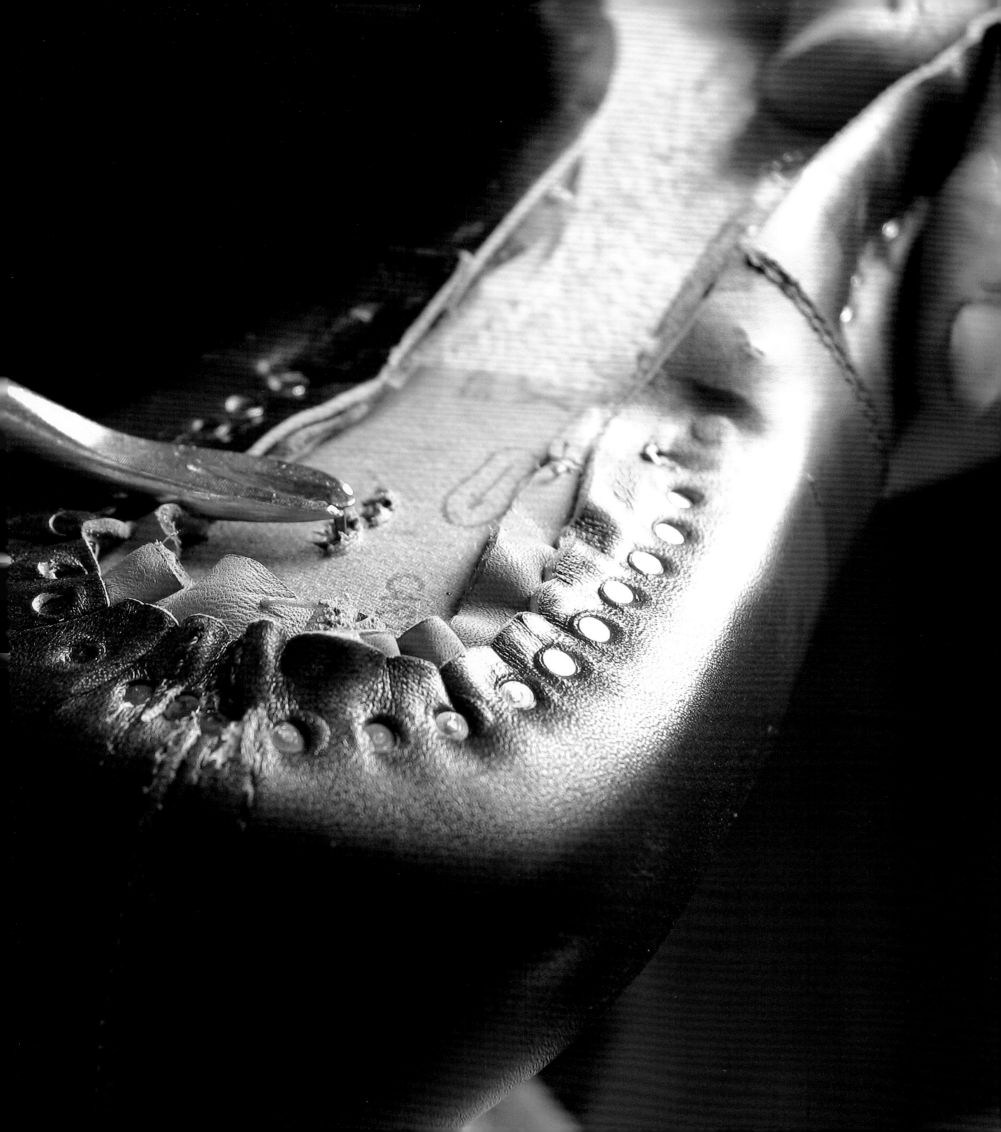

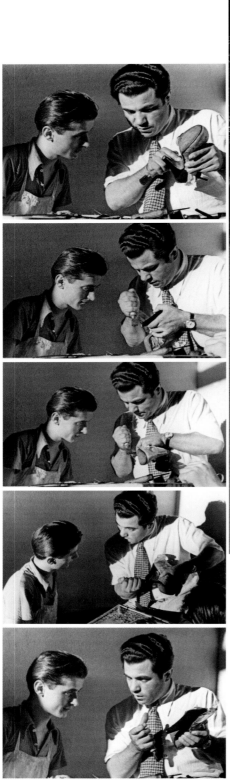

Salvatore Ferragamo
showing one of his
younger employees
how to make a shoe.

萨尔瓦托勒·菲拉格慕向
一位年轻的员工示范如何
制鞋。萨尔瓦托勒·菲拉
格慕档案，佛罗伦萨。

Ferragamo's workshop in Palazzo Spini Feroni, 1937.

菲拉格慕在Palazzo Spini Feroni的工场，1937年。

Shoe manufacturing
phases.

制鞋工序。

"I constructed my revolutionary lasts which, by supporting the arch, make the foot act like an inverted pendulum." (from *Shoemaker of Dreams. The Autobiography of Salvatore Ferragamo*)

"我创造出一种具革命性创新的鞋楦；这鞋楦通过支撑脚拱，令脚的活动变得像一个倒置的钟摆形状。"（摘自萨尔瓦托勒·菲拉格慕的《梦鞋匠》）

Comfort | 舒适感受

Ever since starting out, Salvatore Ferragamo had been obsessed with a problem that for centuries had afflicted those who made shoes by hand and that also seemed critical in the industrial production of the period: to make shoes not only beautiful but comfortable too. This was why Ferragamo went to the States, in the hope of finding a solution. While he was in California, he attended human anatomy courses at the local university, and then found the first clue to the problem in distributing body weight over the arch of the foot. He patented an internal support made of steel, the shank, that shoemakers usually made of thick cardboard or leather. This enabled Ferragamo shoes to become lightweight but strong. This early discovery was followed up by a series of studies of shoe fits that led to his devising of an original system of fitting that also closed the gap between industrial production and made-to-measure shoemaking. The concept was further developed following Ferragamo's death, when artisan production took on its current form, reaching 133 pairs of women's shoes and 110 pairs of men's (per model), in sizes ranging from 3 to 12 for women and 4 to 12 for men and with breadth of sole values from the narrowest to the widest.

This concept of comfort in footwear subsequently became a key value, standing for functionality and wellbeing, in other product categories too.

如何制作出既美观优雅又舒适合脚的鞋履是数百年来一直困扰着手工制鞋匠们的难题，这同样对当时的工业化生产意义攸关。从跻身制鞋行业之初，萨尔瓦托勒·菲拉格慕就为解决这个难题而孜孜以求，这也正是他前往美国的原因—希望能在那里找到解决的办法。在加利福尼亚期间，菲拉格慕曾在当地的大学学习人体解剖课程，从中获得了解决这个难题的第一道启迪：人体的重量集中在双脚的足弓之上。菲拉格慕一改通常鞋匠们选用的厚纸板或厚皮革，而使用钢质鞋芯垫片作为内部支撑结构，并为此申请了专利。这项发明使菲拉格慕的鞋品既轻盈又坚固。继这项早期的发明之后，菲拉格慕又对鞋履的合脚性进行了一系列研究，最终创造了全新的合脚丈量系统，拉近了鞋履的工业化生产和量身订制之间的距离。在菲拉格慕逝世之后，这一概念得到进一步发展，随着现代化制作工艺逐渐形成，公司产量达到了女鞋每款133双和男鞋每款110双，而且尺码齐全，包括女鞋3-12码和男鞋4-12码，并且鞋底规格从瘦到肥应有尽有。

追求鞋品穿着舒适感受这一理念代表着优越的功能性并有益于身体健康，随即成为一个重要的价值观，这在其他产品类别中也逐渐盛行。

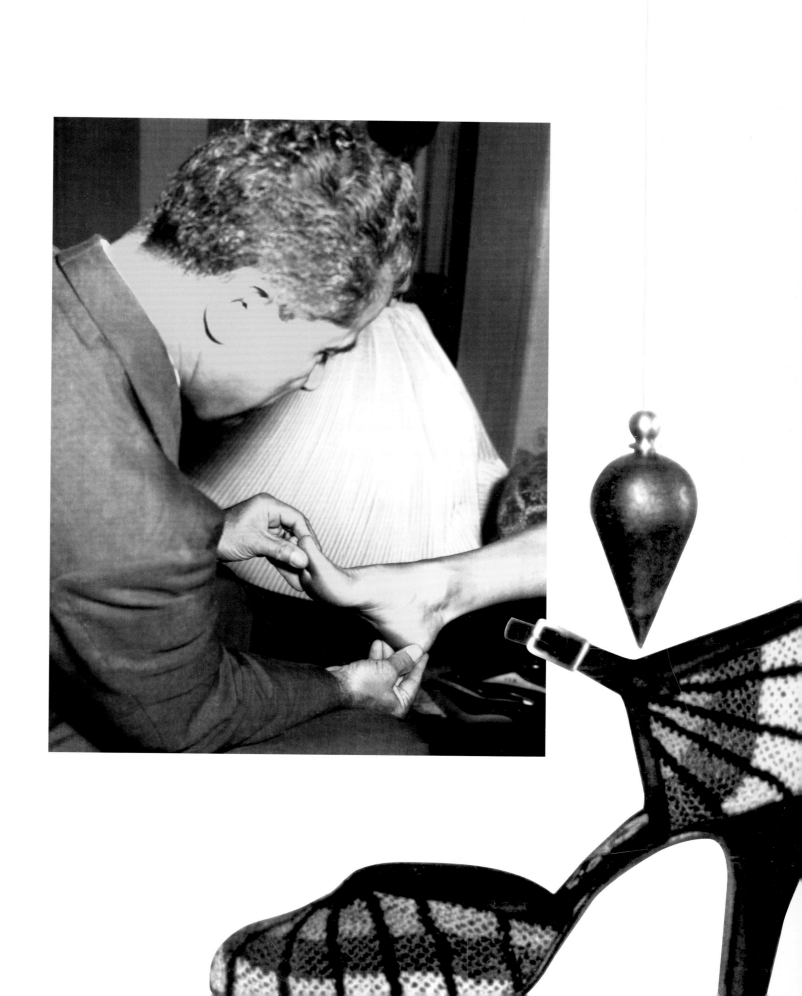

Salvatore Ferragamo touches the arch of a customer's foot before starting to measure. Photo Locchi Archives, Florence.

"I discovered", wrote Salvatore Ferragamo, "that the weight of the body when standing drops vertically on the arches of the feet, as the plum-line shows."

萨尔瓦托勒·菲拉格慕在量尺寸之前首先触摸顾客的足弓。《Locchi摄影纪事》，佛罗伦萨。

"我发现，"萨尔瓦托勒·菲拉格慕写道："当我们垂直站立时，我们的体重像铅垂线一样垂直落在足弓上。"萨尔瓦托勒·菲拉格慕档案资料。

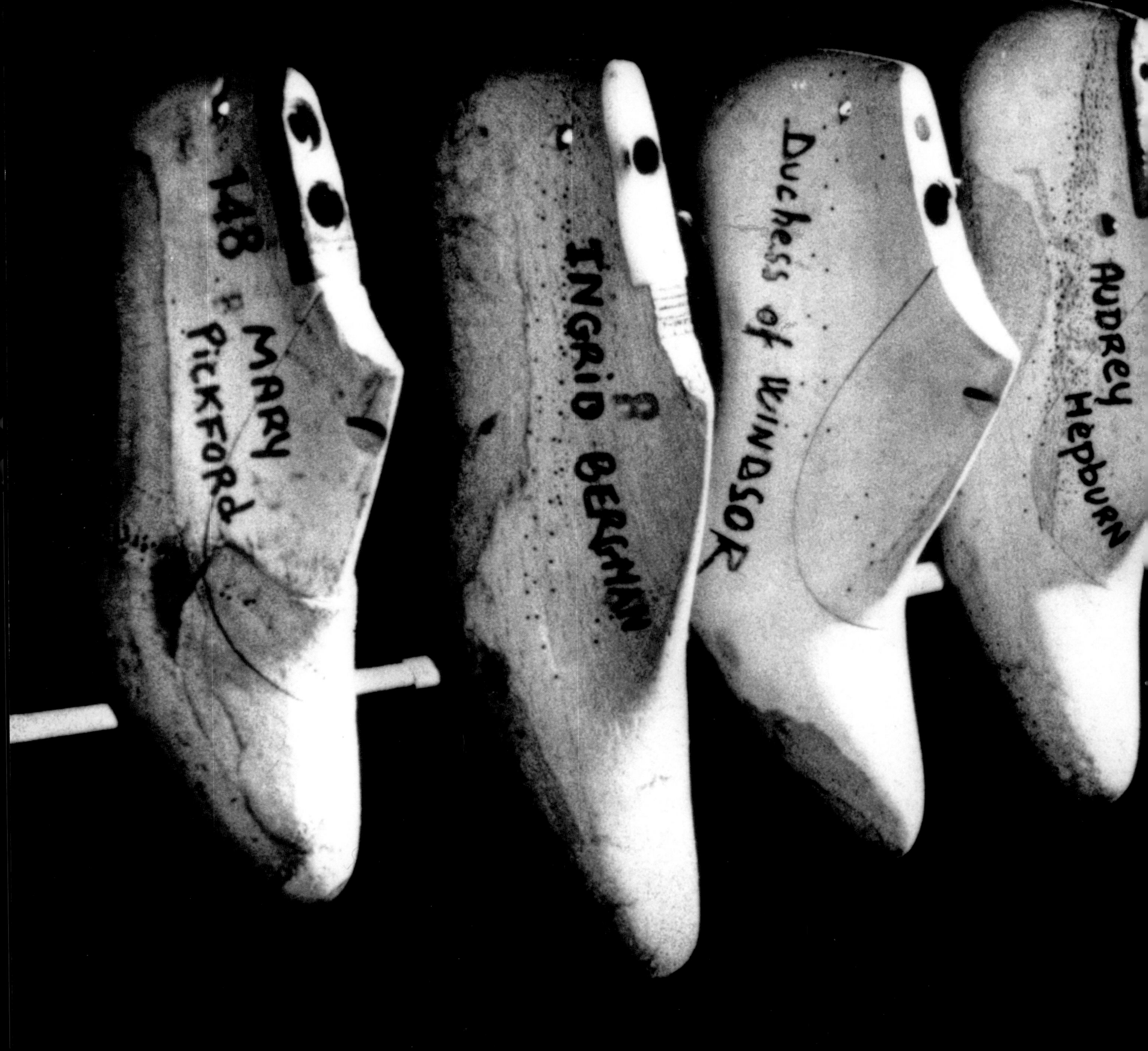
148
MARY PICKFORD
INGRID BERGMAN
Duchess of WINDSOR
AUDREY Hepburn

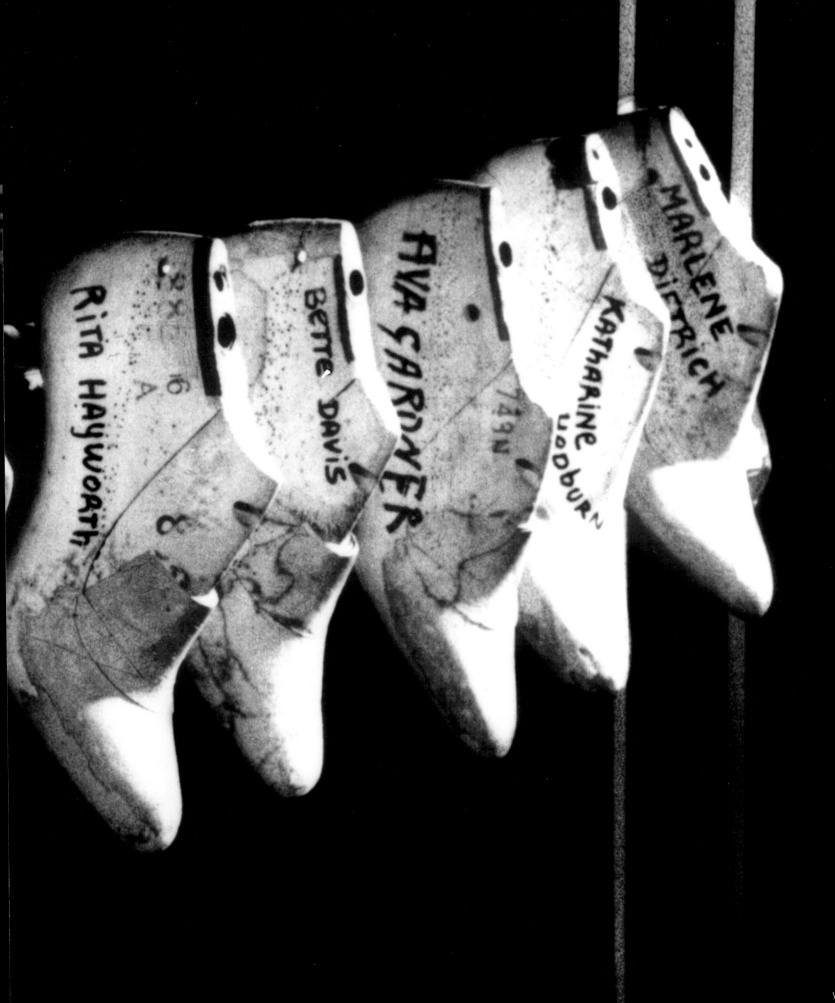

Wooden lasts of the feet
of the famous in Palazzo
Spini Feroni.

Palazzo Spini Feroni中保
存的名人脚形木质鞋楦。

"There is no limit to beauty, no saturation point in design, no end to the materials a shoemaker may use to decorate his creations so that every woman may be shod like a princess and a princess may be shod like a fairy queen." (from *Shoemaker of Dreams. The Autobiography of Salvatore Ferragamo*)

"美丽无极限，设计无止境。鞋匠能采用无穷无尽的物料来装饰自己的设计，让穿上他的鞋子的每一位女性，都可以美丽得像个公主；每一位公主则美丽得像仙境里的皇后一样。"（摘自萨尔瓦托勒·菲拉格慕的《梦鞋匠》）

Materials

材质

Love of materials was a constant in the work of Salvatore Ferragamo and constitutes an invaluable heritage for today's company. Materials, on which the beauty, comfort and durability of a shoe depend as much as on its shape or craftsmanship, were the object of meticulous study for Salvatore. He sought to maintain, indeed enhance, their character whilst adapting them at the same time to the model they were being used for.

This fascination and continual experimentation involved not only traditional and prestige leathers but also more humble or unusual materials. Before and during the Second World War classic Florentine lace, paper, tree bark, raffia, hemp, fish skin and cellophane replaced suppler kidskin and calfskin and exotic crocodile. Immediately after the war, unique and unrepeatable designs for shoe uppers were made possible by new technical developments involving materials like nylon or synthetic raffia and sophisticated embroidery with rhinestones and glass beads (for evening wear).

对材质的热爱是萨尔瓦托勒·菲拉格慕作品永恒的追求，也构成了公司今日无比珍贵的瑰宝和传统。材质，与款形或工艺一样，作为制作优美、舒适、耐久鞋履的基础，是萨尔瓦托勒·菲拉格慕孜孜不倦研究的对象。因此，在根据鞋款选材时，他追求材质特性的保持，甚至提升。

这份热衷的爱和持之以恒的试验不单单局限于长久以来广泛使用的传统皮革，而且也包括许多相对廉价或并非常用的材料。二战爆发前和爆发期间，品质精良的佛罗伦萨蕾丝、纸张、树皮、酒椰、纤维、鱼皮和玻璃纸代替了柔软的小山羊皮、小牛皮和珍贵的鳄鱼皮。战后不久，随着新技术的发展，很多如尼龙、合成酒椰纤维等材料以及镶嵌莱茵石与玻璃彩石（晚装鞋款）的精密刺绣工艺得到应用，从而使独特非凡、无与伦比的鞋帮设计得以实现。

Hand crocheted *Marisa* tote in cotton with perforated leather details. Spring/Summer 2007.

手工钩织的棉质"Marisa"手提包，饰有镂空花纹的皮革。2007年春夏系列。

Prestige Leather

名贵皮革

Brown suede jacket
with pony skin lace.
Spring/Summer 2003–4.

褐色绒面革夹克，饰有小
马皮花边。2003-2004年
春夏系列。

Court shoe in brown
crocodile with stiletto
heel created for Marilyn
Monroe. 1958–59.

为玛丽莲·梦露（Marilyn
Monroe）设计的褐色鳄鱼
皮无带细高跟鞋，
1958-1959年。

Fish Skin 鱼皮

During the 1920s sea leathers were invented. These were the skins of fish prepared in a special way. Since 1928, Salvatore Ferragamo had used the sea-leopard skin, a fish found in Northern waters. In 1954 he reintroduced it after signing an agreement with the Sipo Trading Company, distributors in Denmark.

二十世纪20年代，人们开始使用海产皮革，即通过特殊方式处理鱼皮。
早在1928年，萨尔瓦托勒·菲拉格慕就开始使用产自北部海域的海豹皮。而在1954年，在与一家丹麦经销商—Sipo贸易公司签订供货协议后，菲拉格慕再次开始使用这种特别的皮质。

Court shoe with upper
in dentex skin. 1930–35.

Sea-leopard skins.

Laced shoe with upper
in dentex skin. 1930.

Sea-leopard skins.

海鲷皮鞋帮无带高跟鞋。
1930-1935年。

海豹皮。

海鲷皮鞋帮系带皮鞋。
1930年。

海豹皮。

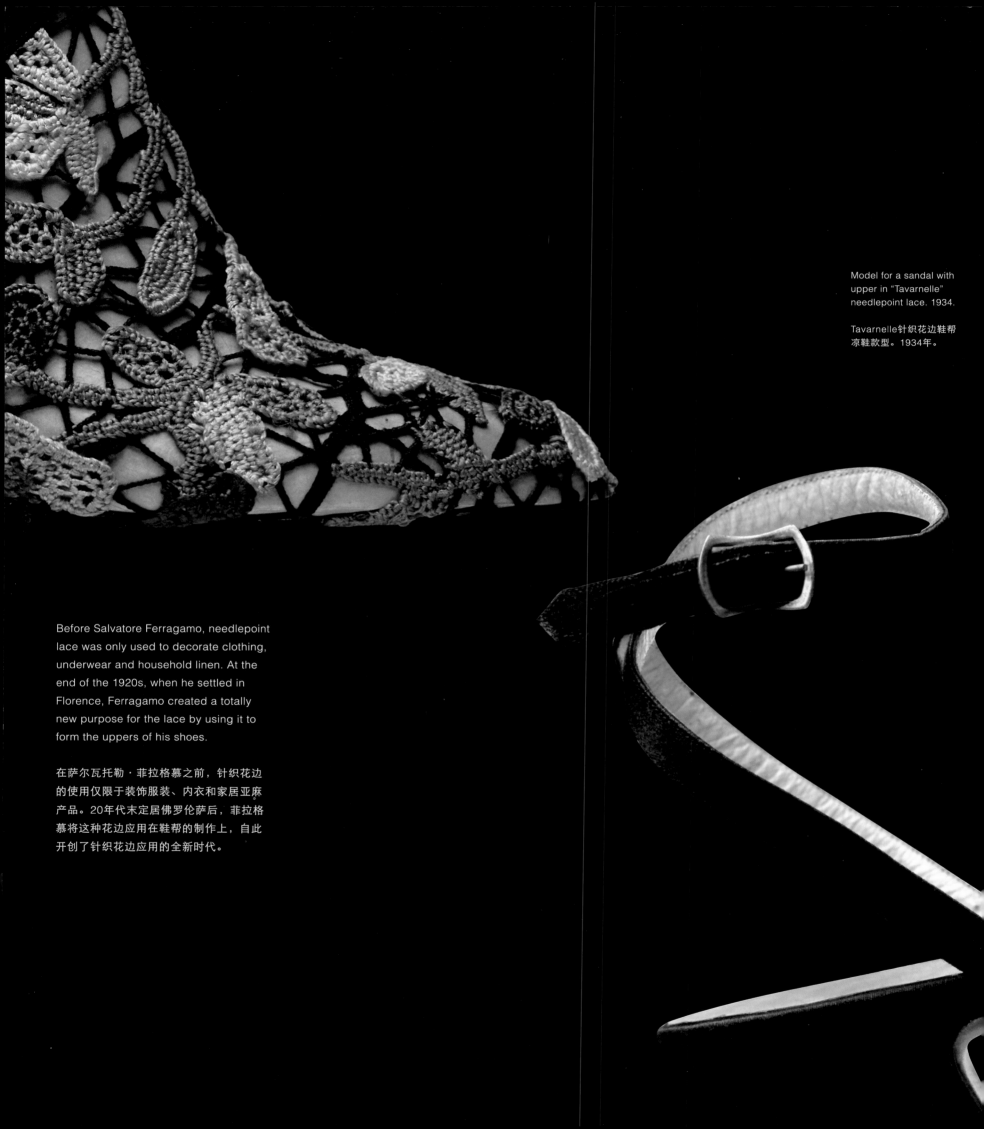

Model for a sandal with
upper in "Tavarnelle"
needlepoint lace. 1934.

Tavarnelle针织花边鞋帮
凉鞋款型。1934年。

Before Salvatore Ferragamo, needlepoint
lace was only used to decorate clothing,
underwear and household linen. At the
end of the 1920s, when he settled in
Florence, Ferragamo created a totally
new purpose for the lace by using it to
form the uppers of his shoes.

在萨尔瓦托勒·菲拉格慕之前，针织花边
的使用仅限于装饰服装、内衣和家居亚麻
产品。20年代末定居佛罗伦萨后，菲拉格
慕将这种花边应用在鞋帮的制作上，自此
开创了针织花边应用的全新时代。

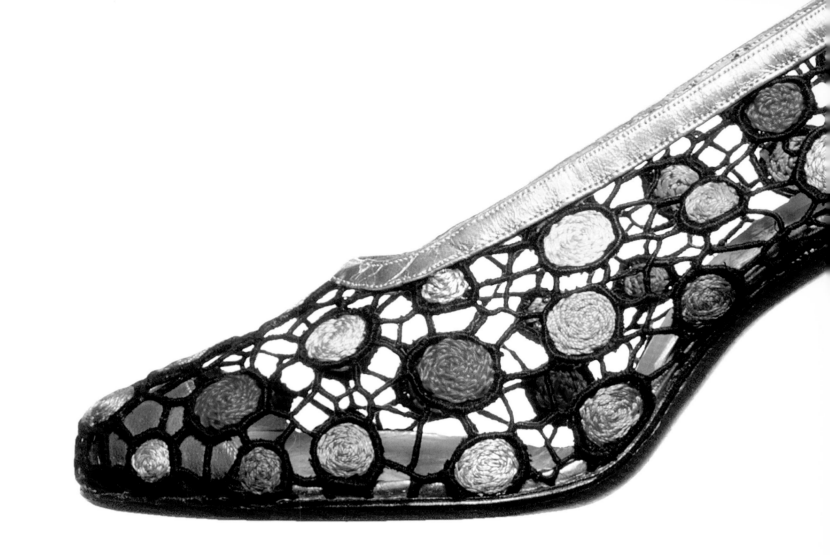

Iride court shoe. Upper in kid, "Tavarnelle" needlepoint lace embroidered with small circles. 1935–36.

Sandal with upper in satin and "Tavarnelle" needlepoint lace. 1935.

无带高跟鞋。小山羊皮鞋帮，点缀小巧圆形刺绣Tavarnelle针织花边。1935-1936年。

绸缎面料带Tavarnelle针织花边鞋帮凉鞋。1935年。

Embroideries and Needlepoint Laces

刺绣和针织花边

Michouette and *Vivia* models in satin embroidered with Venetian beads, stones and strass. 1968.

"Michouette"和"Vivia"款型，绸缎面料，镶嵌威尼斯玻璃珠、宝石和水晶玻璃。1968年。

Sandal with Venetian
glass beads and strass
embroidered upper.
1956.

镶嵌威尼斯玻璃珠和水晶
玻璃鞋帮凉鞋。1956年。

Straw and Raffia

稻草和酒椰纤维

When Ferragamo settled in Florence, straw manufacture, one of the city's most thriving activities, inspired him revive the use of this traditional material in shoes. The finished straw was sold in the straw market in Florence.

菲拉格慕定居佛罗伦萨后，当地繁荣兴盛的草制品业激励他将这一传统材料重新应用于制鞋。
经过加工的稻草在佛罗伦萨的稻草市场有售。

The raffia embroidered upper of a 1938 sandal.

1938年款凉鞋系列，
刺绣酒椰鞋帮。

Sandal with upper in woven grass from the Philippines. 1938.

Sandal with upper in woven raffia and cork wedge heel. 1938–40.

菲律宾产稻草编织鞋帮凉鞋。1938年。

酒椰编鞋帮凉鞋，软木楔形鞋跟。1938-1940年。

Cheap Materials

低廉的材料

"The shoes", wrote Salvatore Ferragamo, "are bought plain and taken to an artist who will paint on them the designs of your choice."

"人们购买了平朴的鞋子，"萨尔瓦托勒·菲拉格慕写道："然后带给艺术家，让他们在上面绘制顾客精选的设计图案。"

Prototype sandal with upper in natural hemp and plaited cords of multicoloured cotton. 1936–38.

Model for a mule with upper in felt decorated with cotton ribbons. 1938.

饰有彩色棉质褶皱的天然纤维鞋帮凉鞋原型款。1936-1938年。

饰有棉质细条的毛毡鞋帮凉拖鞋款型。1938年。

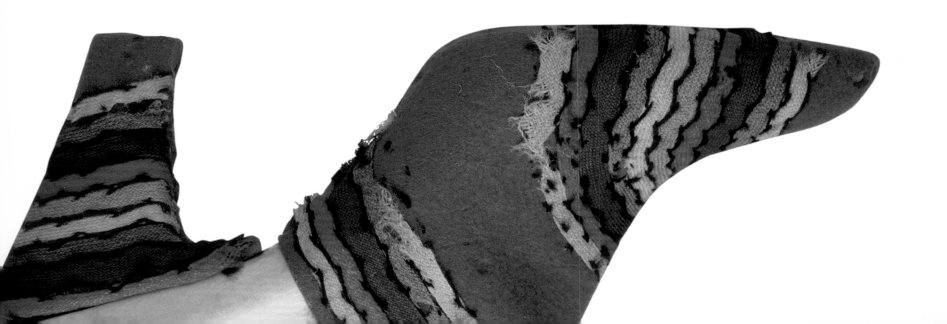

Laced boot with hand-painted canvas. 1930.

Hand-painted canvas upper. 1930.

手绘帆布面料系带皮靴。 1930年。

手绘帆布鞋帮。1930年。

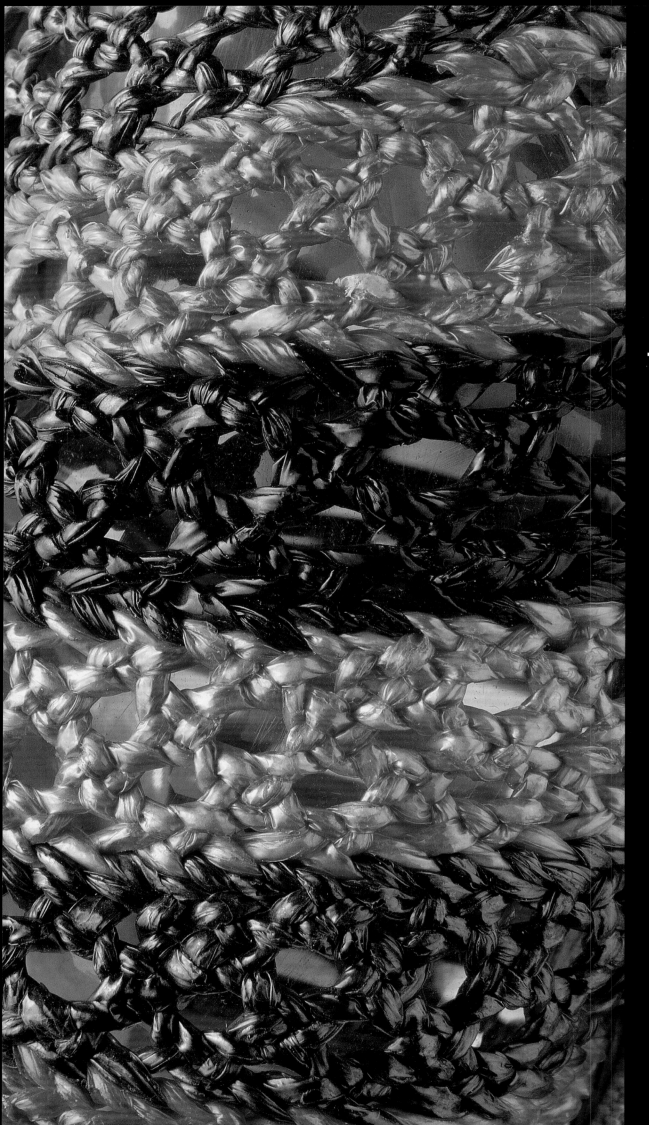

Cellophane and Plastics 玻璃纸和塑料

"During the war", Salvatore Ferragamo wrote, "my first major problem was to find a substitute for the fine quality kid-skins. Then, one Sunday morning, I found the solution. My mother was extremely fond of chocolates, and this day I bought a box back to the house. As I unwrapped a chocolate for her I was attracted by its transparent paper wrapping. Here might be the substitute I was seeking." This marked the beginning of Ferragamo's production of shoes in cellophane to provide elegant summer wear.

萨尔瓦托勒·菲拉格慕写道："战争时期，我的第一个主要难题，就是要寻找能替代优质小山羊皮的物料；结果，在某个星期天早上，我找到了答案。家母十分喜欢吃巧克力。这一天我买了一盒回家。替母亲打开盒子的时候，我被那用来包装的透明纸吸引住了。心想这也许正是我在找的替代品。"这标志着菲拉格慕使用玻璃纸为材料制作高雅凉鞋的开端。

Chrocheted cellophane upper. 1942–44.

钩织玻璃纸鞋面。
1942-1944年。

Mule with upper in vinyl and kid. Heel in Plexiglas. 1952–54.

Laced shoe with woven cellophane upper. High heel covered with kid. 1941–42.

乙烯基材料和小山羊皮鞋帮凉拖鞋。树脂玻璃鞋跟。1952-1954年。

编织玻璃纸鞋帮系带高跟鞋，鞋跟外包小山羊皮。1941-1942年。

"How else can I explain my sense of design? I do not have to search for styles. When I need new ones, I do select from those that present themselves to my mind as I select an apple from the laden dish upon my table. Today there are more than 20,000 models in my shoe library, and I hold more than 350 patents, some of which have been used and some of which are still waiting to be used." (from *Shoemaker of Dreams. The Autobiography of Salvatore Ferragamo*)

"还有什么方法能解释我的设计触觉？我根本不必为鞋子的款式而思索。当我要设计新款式的时候，它们便会从我脑海里自动跑出来，我只消从中挑选一个，就像从满载水果的盘子上挑出一个苹果似的。今天在我的鞋子收藏馆里，便收藏了二万多款我的设计，我还拥有超过三百五十项设计专利，当中有些已被采用，有些正等着被采用。"（摘自萨尔瓦托勒·菲拉格慕的《梦鞋匠》）

Inventions and Symbols

创新与标志

Salvatore Ferragamo was a great innovator in the style and fashion of footwear design. Like the big names in industrial design, he invented new forms basing himself on functional needs that defined appearance, such as the cork wedge (1937) designed to give the heel stability and which then became the hallmark of an epoch. Ever alert to the contemporary scene, he was particularly interested in art, design and architecture. The shoe he created in 1939 with a high, mosaic heel reminds us of the taste widespread in the 1930s for mosaics in buildings or private interiors. In the 1950s, Ferragamo's creativity contributed to the success of Italian design and fashion with inventions that changed the history of footwear and which are still sources of inspiration for stylists today: from the "invisible" sandal (1947) to the moulded arch (1952), from the cage heel (1955) to the seashell sole.
Salvatore's creativity was perpetuated in the work of his children and in particular Fiamma, who invented a number of shoes and accessories that were to become the most recognisable emblems of the brand.

萨尔瓦托勒·菲拉格慕是鞋品设计风格与时尚的卓越创新者。正如工业设计领域中许多大名鼎鼎的发明家一样，菲拉格慕从功能性需求出发，定义鞋品的外观，不断创造出崭新的鞋品款形。例如他于1937年设计的软木楔形鞋跟不仅带来了稳健、舒适的穿着感受，而且成为了那个时代极为风靡的标志性款式。菲拉格慕密切关注时代潮流的发展趋势，尤其痴迷于艺术、设计和建筑学。他于1939年设计的嵌花高跟女鞋，让人不由联想起上世纪30年代建筑或室内装潢中马赛克工艺的神韵。而50年代期间，菲拉格慕的创作才华为意大利的设计和时尚界做出了巨大贡献，从1947年的"隐形"凉鞋，到1952年的铸模鞋拱，从1955年的笼形鞋跟到贝壳形鞋底，他的一系列创新杰作不仅对鞋品的发展历史产生了深远影响，直至今天仍源源不断地为当代时尚设计提供着灵感。
萨尔瓦托勒的设计创造力，在他子女们的不懈努力下延续着新的传奇；尤其是菲安玛在鞋品、配件设计上的多项创新，成为了该品牌最受赞誉的标志性作品。

Arch

隐蔽鞋拱

Patent 41888, 7 July 1952. In 1952 Ferragamo designed a high-heeled shoe, in which the arch of the foot was lined with the same leather as the upper, limiting the sole to the front and heel. The model proved to be tough but flexible, like a glove, and the patent was known as the "gloved arch".

Court shoe with rust calf upper. High heel in wood and arch covered in calf. Top piece and forepart sole in leather. 1950.

专利第41888号，1952年7月7日。高跟鞋，菲拉格幕于1952年设计，其鞋拱部分衬以与鞋帮相同的皮革，而仅有前脚和后跟部分保留鞋底。该款型不仅结实，而且如手套般柔软，其专利取名为"隐蔽鞋拱"。

深褐色小牛皮鞋帮的无带女鞋。木质高跟、鞋拱包裹以小牛皮。皮革材质鞋垫和前脚鞋底，1950年。

The cork wedge, which has generated a number of new models over the years, is one of the most recognisable of Ferragamo symbols and originated in an autarkic period to answer a specific functional need, that of replacing the steel plate Ferragamo had patented in the 1920s to support the arch of the foot.

Without the right sort of steel, which Ferragamo used to import from Germany and which he could no longer purchase due to the economic sanctions against Italy, Ferragamo shoe construction was bereft of one of its main elements.

"I started working with bits of Sardinian cork", wrote Salvatore, "pressing it, gluing it, fixing and finishing it till the space between sole and heel was filled up".

This was the birth of the wedge, destined to be one of the most famous fashion inventions of the 1940s. The Duchessa Visconti di Modrone had the honour of launching the first pair. Within a few weeks it became Salvatore Ferragamo's most popular model.

The wedge enabled the creativity of an artist like Ferragamo to express itself on surfaces more ample than those of uppers and heel alone. He experimented with many variants on the wedge, both platform and heel, with layers pressed and rounded, sculpted and painted, decorated with bits of mirror glass like an antique mosaic or with floral patterned brass latticework spattered with stones. Such creations had more in common with contemporary design or with architectures such as the Chrysler Building in New York than with the fashion accessories of the moment.

多年以来，软木楔形鞋跟已衍生出众多款式新颖的鞋品，是菲拉格慕最鲜明的标志性风格之一。而它的产生源于一段经济闭塞的时期：菲拉格慕在制鞋中采用一种薄钢片对足弓加以支撑，这是他在20年代获得的一项专利技术；然而，由于意大利受到经济制裁，原本依赖于从德国采购并进口的薄钢片无法保证供应，菲拉格慕制鞋面临着缺乏主要制作原料的难题。为了缓解这一特殊的功能性需求，寻求替代技术，菲拉格慕由此创造了软木楔跟。

"我开始使用一些撒丁岛软木制作鞋跟，"菲拉格慕写道："将其压实、胶合、固定并对表面加以装饰，直到鞋底与鞋跟之间的空间完全填满为止。"

此为楔形鞋跟的诞生历史，它注定将成为四十年代最闻名于世的时尚创作之一！Visconti di Modrone公爵夫人有幸穿上了第一双楔跟鞋品。短短数周内，该款鞋品就成为萨尔瓦托勒·菲拉格慕最受欢迎的款式。

楔形鞋跟为菲拉格慕这样的艺术大师尽情展示自己无限的创造力开拓了更广阔的空间，单单从鞋帮或鞋跟着手是远远不够的。

菲拉格慕对楔形鞋跟，包括厚鞋底和鞋根的设计进行过多种改款尝试，例如将多层软木经过压实、修圆、雕刻并上色，饰以小块银色镜面，营造出类似仿古马赛克效果，或装饰以带有花卉图案的黄铜网条并点缀以宝石。与当时的时尚配件相比，这些创意倒与现代设计或者像纽约克莱斯勒大厦那样的建筑更加神似。

楔跟的灵感

Sandal with kid upper. Platform sole and heel with layers of cork lined with different coloured suede. This sandal was made for Judy Garland in 1938.

小山羊皮鞋帮凉鞋。厚鞋底，鞋根由多层软木外包不同色泽的绒面革制成。这款凉鞋专为朱迪·嘉兰（Judy Garland）设计制作。1938年。

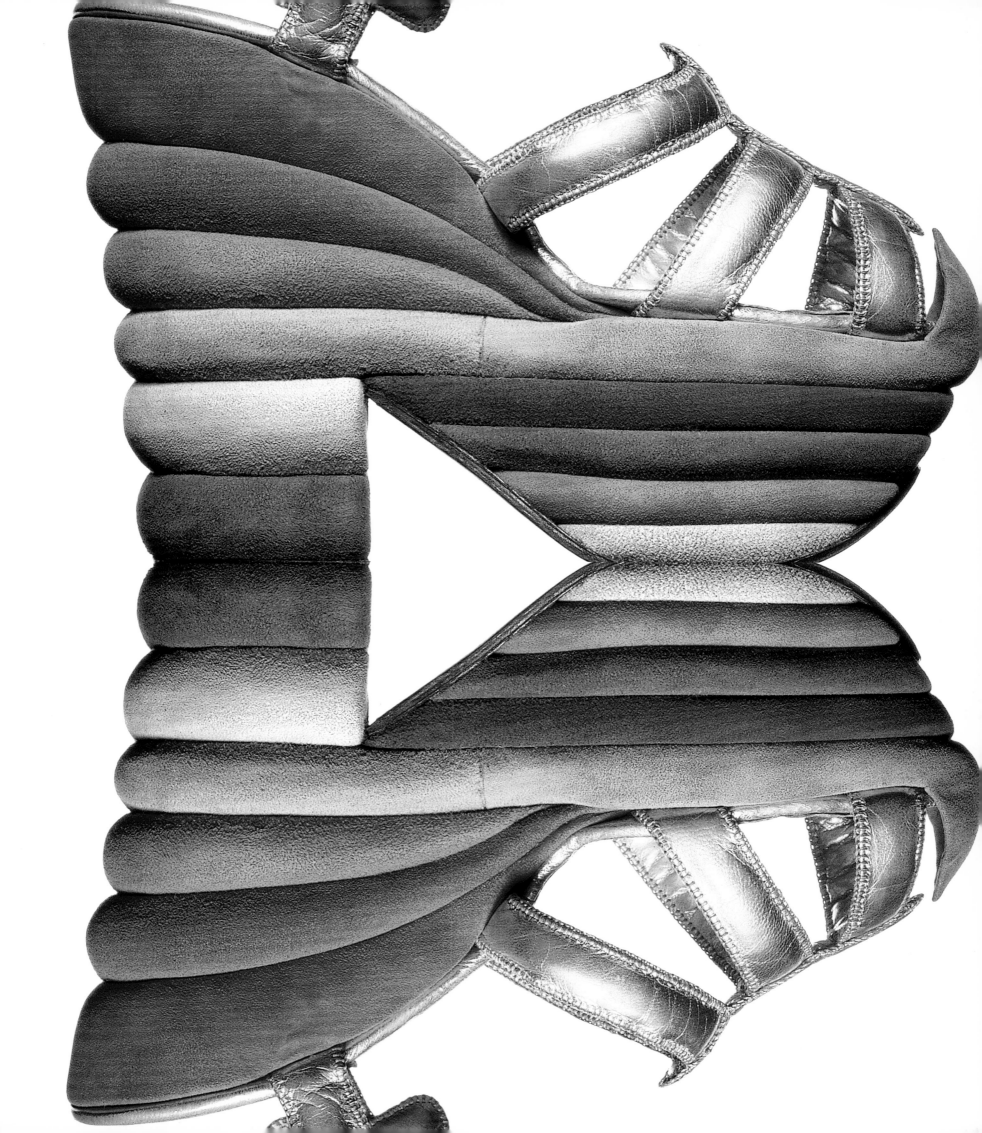

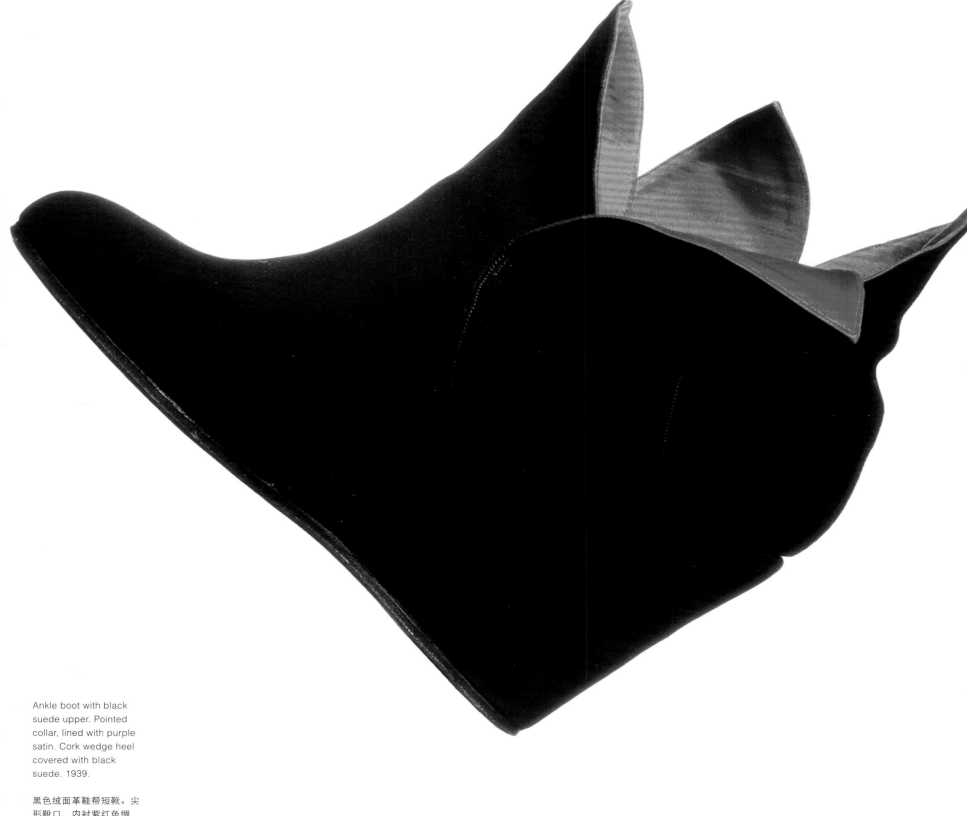

Ankle boot with black
suede upper. Pointed
collar, lined with purple
satin. Cork wedge heel
covered with black
suede. 1939.

黑色绒面革鞋帮短靴。尖
形靴口，内衬紫红色绸
缎。软木楔形鞋跟，外包
黑色绒面革。1939年。

Sandal in satin purple
and gold kid. Wedge
heel in layers of cork
covered with satin and
kid. 1936–38.

紫红色绸缎和金色小山羊
皮面料凉鞋。多层软木楔
形鞋跟，外包绸缎和小山
羊皮。1936-1938年。

Sandal with black velvet and silver kid upper. Wood flat-through sole joining high heel to cork platform sole covered with strips of silver and gold kid. 1939–40.

Sandal with the upper made up of black satin. Wedge platform and heel made up of four convex layers of cork covered with alternate gilt and silver calf. 1938.

Bray sandal with upper in brown velvet. Gilt platform and heel, inspired to the 1938 wedge. Fall/Winter 2005–6.

Patent 15953, 10 March 1939. Sole for shoes, sandals and the like, made up of several layers of cork wrapped with fabric.

黑色天鹅绒和银色小山羊皮面料凉鞋。木质平鞋底，外包银色小山羊皮，将外包银色小山羊皮的高跟与外包银色和金色小山羊皮皮条的软木厚鞋底相连。1939-40年。

黑色绸缎鞋帮凉鞋。楔形厚鞋底；鞋跟由四层凸面软木交替外包金、银色小牛皮制成。1938年。

"Bray"。褐色天鹅绒鞋帮凉鞋。金色厚鞋底和鞋跟，灵感来源于1938年的楔形鞋底。2005-2006年秋冬系列。

专利第15953号，1939年3月10日。鞋底，由多层软木外包面料制成，用于制作皮鞋、凉鞋等。

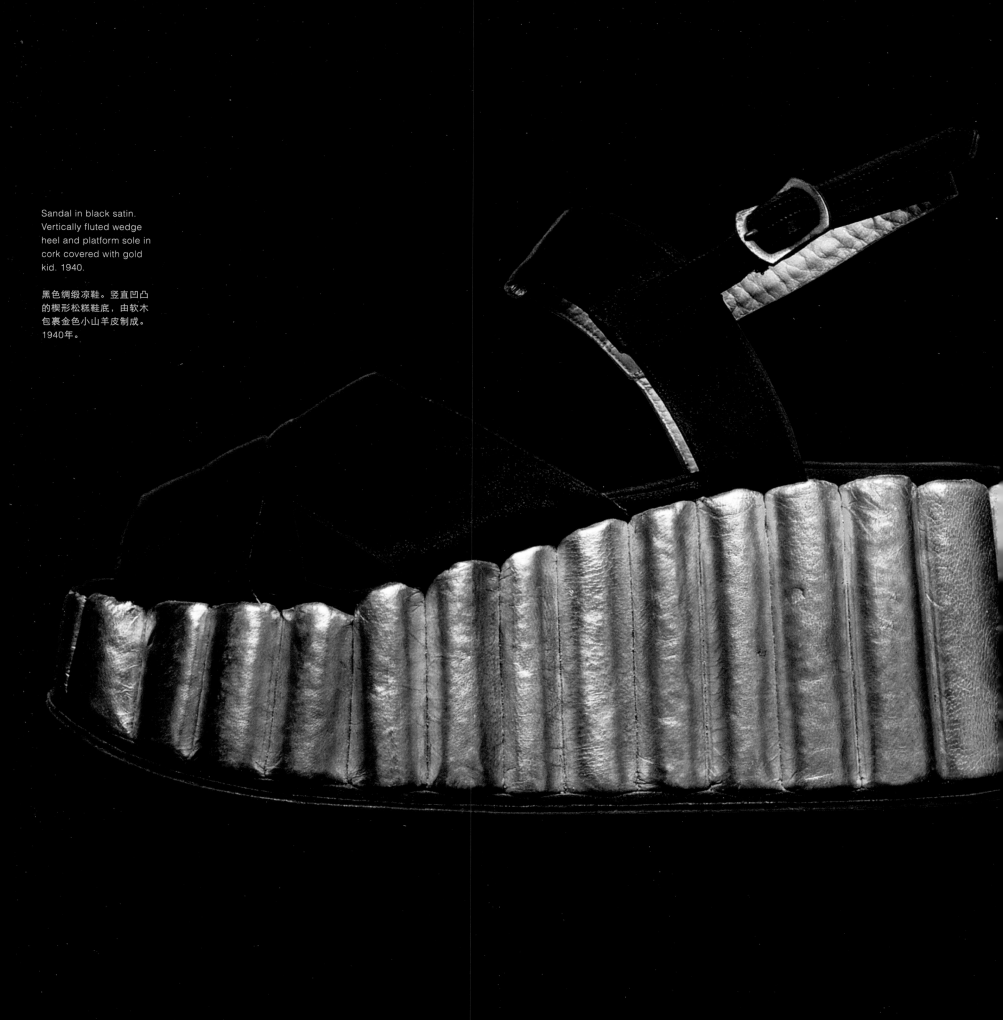

Sandal in black satin.
Vertically fluted wedge
heel and platform sole in
cork covered with gold
kid. 1940.

黑色绸缎凉鞋。竖直凹凸
的楔形松糕鞋底，由软木
包裹金色小山羊皮制成。
1940年。

Sandal with vamp comprising two strips of black satin and gold kid. A mosaic of small gilded mirrors glued to waxed canvas covers the cork platform sole and heel. Gold kid insole edge cover. Black satin lining and sock. Leather sole. This sandal was created for Carmen Miranda in 1938.

凉鞋，鞋帮由两条黑色绸缎和金色小山羊皮相间的带子构成。软木厚鞋底和鞋跟上包有涂蜡帆布，外贴镀金马赛克。鞋的内底饰有金色小山羊皮包边。黑色绸缎衬里和软垫。皮革鞋底。这款凉鞋专为卡门·米兰达（Carmen Miranda）设计制作。1938年。

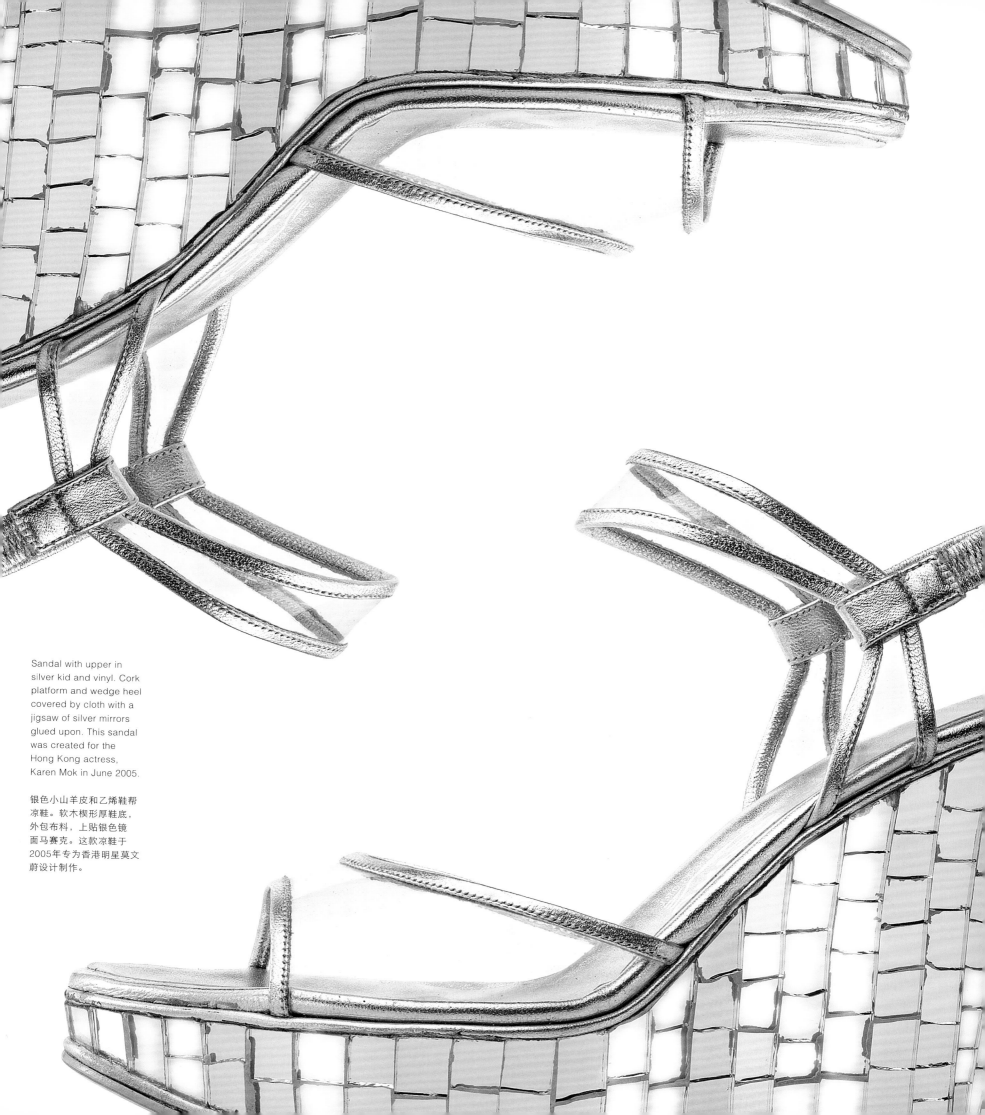

Sandal with upper in
silver kid and vinyl. Cork
platform and wedge heel
covered by cloth with a
jigsaw of silver mirrors
glued upon. This sandal
was created for the
Hong Kong actress,
Karen Mok in June 2005.

银色小山羊皮和乙烯鞋帮
凉鞋。软木楔形厚鞋底，
外包布料，上贴银色镜
面马赛克。这款凉鞋于
2005年专为香港明星莫文
蔚设计制作。

Maharani 凉鞋

One of Salvatore Ferragamo's most famous customers in the late 1930s was Indira Devi, the Maharani of Cooch Behar. This Indian princess ordered even a hundred pairs of shoes at a time, some of them adorned with real pearls and diamonds.

In 1938 Salvatore Ferragamo created a pair of sandals for her with uppers composed of bands of kid and satin sewn together, a cork wedge (his latest invention) covered in velvet and embossed brass structure embedded with precious gems – rubies, emeralds, diamonds and other stones – that the Maharani had sent from India.

This extraordinary sandal, made by expert craftsmen who are heirs to Florence's Renaissance artistic tradition, was reproduced in 2003 for the opening of the new Ferragamo flagship store in Ginza, in exclusive for Japan and solely made to order.

This sandal has also inspired a line of exclusive shoes, bags and eyeglasses.

印度库赫·巴哈公主Indira Devi是萨尔瓦托勒·菲拉格慕上世纪三十年代末最显赫的顾客之一。这位尊贵的印度公主甚至一次订购了一百双鞋履，其中一些饰有华贵的珍珠和钻石。

1938年，萨尔瓦托勒·菲拉格慕专门为她制作了一款凉鞋，鞋帮以小山羊皮与绸缎缝制而成的带子构成，软木楔鞋跟（他的最新的创意），外包天鹅绒和浮雕黄铜，上嵌Indira Devi公主从印度寄来的红宝石、翡翠、钻石等各种珍贵宝石。

这款举世无双的凉鞋，由继承了佛罗伦萨文艺复兴时期艺术传统的技艺精湛的制鞋巨匠制作，于2003年为庆祝位于东京银座的新菲拉格慕旗舰店开业重新推出，专供日本市场并仅接受客户预订。

这款凉鞋还是一系列独特别致的鞋品、皮包和太阳镜产品的灵感源泉。

Indira Devi, the Maharani of Cooch Behar in 1934.

The *Maharani* sandal created in 1938 by Salvatore Ferragamo for the Maharani of Cooch Behar.

Indira Devi，印度库赫·巴哈（Cooch Behar）公主，1934年。

"Maharani"凉鞋，由萨尔瓦托勒·菲拉格慕于1938年专为印度库赫·巴哈（Cooch Behar）的公主设计制作。

Maharaja ballet slipper and small evening bag, Minaudière in red satin. A jewelled decoration reproduces the ornamental design of the *Maharani* sandal. May 2003.

"Maharaja" 芭蕾
舞鞋和红色绸缎质地
的 "Minaudière" 晚装手
包。二者华丽的宝石装饰
再现了 "Maharani" 凉鞋
的装饰设计风格。2003年
5月。

Finzia sandal in gold suede strips and gold-tone metal arabesque heel. Fall/Winter 2003–4.

"Finzia"。金色绒面革
细带凉鞋，高跟饰有阿拉
伯风情的金质蔓藤花纹。
2003-2004年秋冬系列。

The Invisible Sandal

"隐形"凉鞋

Salvatore Ferragamo explained in his autobiography, "I took a length of the water-coloured thread and twisted and wound it round the sculpted heel. The result was the *Invisible* shoe, a style which helped to win for me the Neiman Marcus Award. It was never a good selling line, however, because it leaves the foot so naked and so poised that few women dare accept this extreme challenge to the beauty of their feet". The price of $29.75 for a pair of "invisible" sandals would buy four tons of coal. This is one of the most famous items of footwear since the last war. It was shown in Dallas, where it won an award, along with Christian Dior, Irene of Hollywood and Norman Hartnell, and was seen as a symbol of post-war fashion. The F-shape of the wedge heel, being also Ferragamo's initial, became one of the leitmotifs in his collections over the years, a hallmark of his style.

萨尔瓦托勒·菲拉格慕在自传中写道："我拿来一段透明的鱼丝，绕在雕花的鞋跟上，结果就创造出这双让我赢得尼曼—马库斯奖的'隐形'凉鞋。然而它并不畅销，因为令双脚看来极为裸露、悬空，所以少有女性敢让自己的脚接受如此严苛的美感挑战。"
隐形凉鞋高达29.75美元的售价足够买下4吨煤。作为二战以来最负盛名的鞋履之一，该鞋品曾在达拉斯展出并获奖，共同分享该奖的还有克里司汀·迪奥（Christian Dior）、好莱坞的艾琳（Irene）以及诺曼哈特内尔（Norman Hartnell），他们被看作是战后时尚的标志。楔形鞋跟的"F"形造型，也类似菲拉格慕姓氏（Ferragamo）的首字母，是菲拉格慕多年来诸多产品系列经久不衰的设计主题之一，成为了他非凡风格的独特标志。

Invention patent 426001, 17 October 1947. Shoe manufacturing procedure with the upper made out of seamless thread, twine, ribbon and the like.

Galilea sandal with PVC upper and F-shaped wedge heel covered with mother-of-pearl. 2003.

专利第426001号，1947年10月17日。鞋帮以无接头细线、捻纱、缎带等材料制成。

"Galilea"凉鞋，树脂材质鞋帮，F形楔跟，饰有珍珠母贝。2003年。

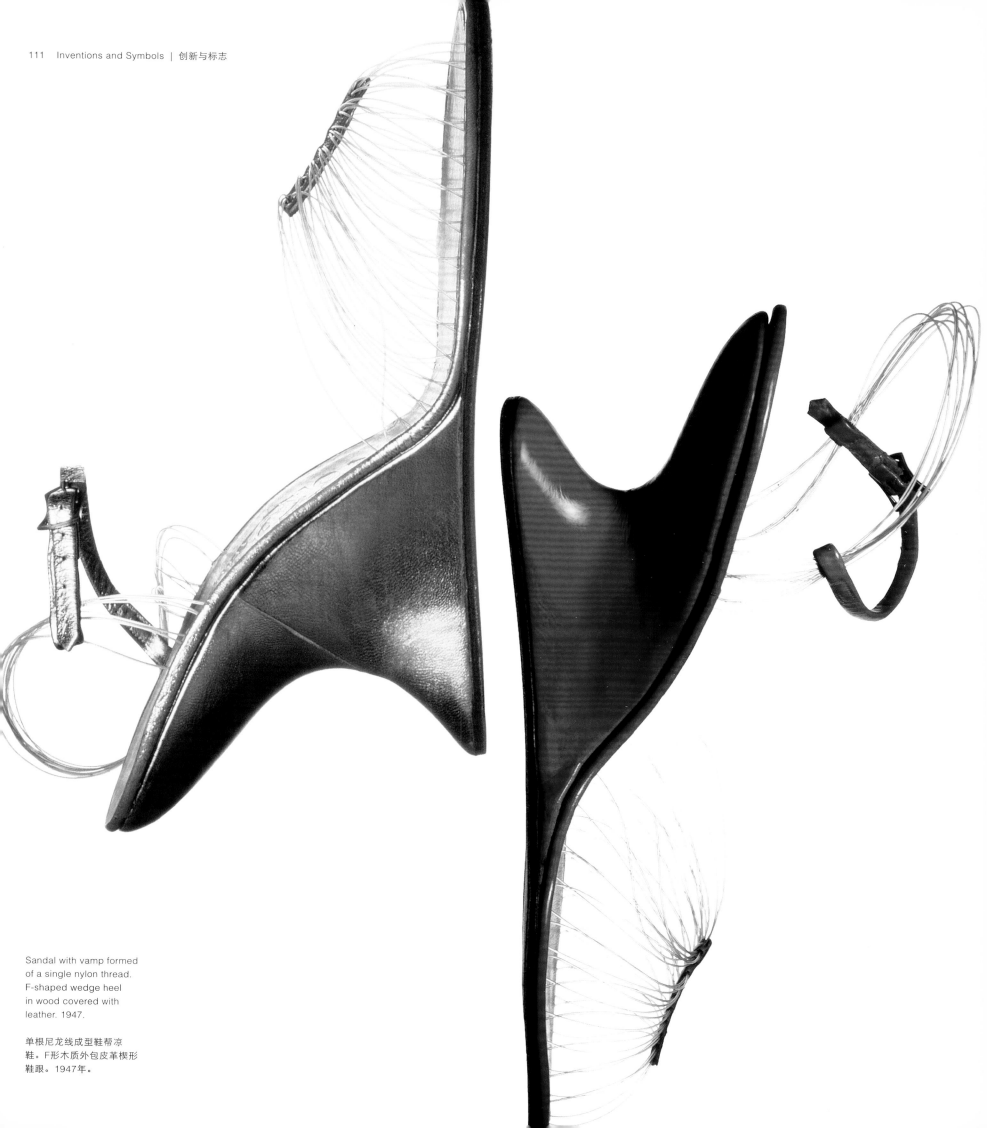

Sandal with vamp formed
of a single nylon thread.
F-shaped wedge heel
in wood covered with
leather. 1947.

单根尼龙线成型鞋帮凉
鞋。F形木质外包皮革楔形
鞋跟。1947年。

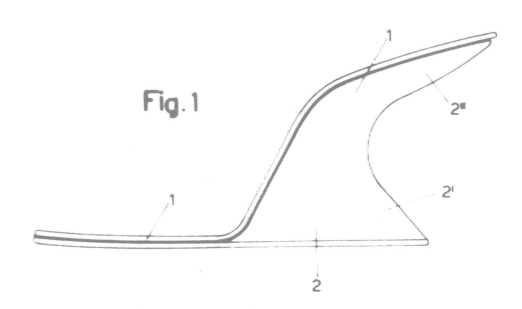

F Heel F 形楔跟

One of Salvatore Ferragamo's most famous patents is the "wedge" heel shaped like the stern of a ship, whose line is obtained by means of a central support and a rear "shelf". In Ferragamo history, it's called the "F heel" because Salvatore created it with the F of his signature in mind.

萨尔瓦托勒·菲拉格慕最著名的专利之一是形状酷似船尾的"楔形"鞋跟，其线条由中央的支撑物和后部的"跟架"构成。在菲拉格慕的历史中，该鞋跟又称为"F"形楔跟，因为萨尔瓦托勒·菲拉格慕先生从自己姓氏的首字母"F"中获得灵感，创造了这一别致的鞋跟。

Fig. 1

Patent 26673, 10 May 1947. Support shape for shoe sole, with central spur and support for the heel.

America sandal with upper in gold kid and PVC. 1947.

专利第26673号，1947年5月10日。鞋底采用支撑设计，鞋跟有中央支柱。

"America"凉鞋，鞋帮采用金色小山羊皮和树脂面料。1947年。

Reply court shoe with open toe. Upper in crocodile. Wedge heel covered with kid. Fall/Winter 2007–8.

Romola court shoe with upper in calf. Wedge heel covered with silver metal. Fall/Winter 2007–8.

"Reply" 露趾宽松高跟鞋，鞋帮采用鳄鱼皮面料。楔形鞋跟外包小山羊皮。2007-2008年秋冬系列。

"Romola" 宽松高跟鞋，鞋帮采用小牛皮面料。楔形鞋跟，饰有银色金属。2007-2008年秋冬系列。

The Shell-Shaped Sole

"贝壳形鞋底"

One of Ferragamo's most important patents was the "shell-shaped sole". This sole was used in a popular range of shoes including slippers, ankle boots, court shoes and even ballet shoes. Borrowed from the pattern of the Indian *opanke*, the moccasin of America's native Indians, in which the sole mounts the heel to become the upper, Ferragamo's shell-shaped sole contained and caressed the foot with its curved, embracing form.

"贝壳形鞋底"是菲拉格慕重要的专利设计之一。这一鞋底造型在多款极受欢迎的鞋履，包括拖鞋、短靴、浅口鞋甚至芭蕾舞鞋上得到了广泛的应用。借鉴美国本土印第安人的平底敞口皮鞋"opanke"的样式 — 后跟装于鞋底上并延伸至鞋帮，菲拉格慕贝壳形鞋底伏贴地包融、契合着脚的曲线，贴合脚的外形。

Invention patent 578173,
20 June 1958.

The *Audrey* model from
1954, still in production
today.

第578173号发明专利，
1958年6月20日。

"奥黛丽"鞋款，诞生
于1954年，至今仍畅销
不衰。

Popular imagination sees feminine seduction in high heels, preferably metallic, aggressive and luminous. Steel or brass heels have graced shoes by Ferragamo since the 1920s, as in the famous model with the pyramid shaped facetted heel inspired by the discovery of the tomb of Tutankhamen in Egypt. But they were at the height of fashion above all in the 1950s.

In 1955 Salvatore Ferragamo filed a number of important patents. One was a metallised heel in various colours, lined with a lamina of aluminium; another was a "cage" heel, hollow and lightweight yet strong. The third, and even more ingenious, patent was for a multiple heel adorned with gem-spattered, gold or silver plated metal decorations painstakingly hand-crafted to look like lacework.

But the most extraordinary invention was the metal sole that Ferragamo patented in 1956, when he was called on to create the most costly shoe he'd ever made – an 18kt gold sandal for an Australian customer, wife of an oil magnate. It was made in collaboration with the Florentine goldsmiths on the Ponte Vecchio, who had to produce special chains to form the uppers and gold plating for the sole and heel, the latter decorated with an embossed dragon. This icon of material wealth and craftsmanship is "quoted" in some of the subsequent evening models such as the *Boreale* sandal of Fall/Winter 2005–6 collection – a haunting masterpiece of the past transformed into an object of contemporary design.

闪耀着金属光泽、张扬不羁而光彩熠熠的纤细高跟，洋溢着柔美的女性魅力，给人以无限遐想。自从上世纪20年代起，菲拉格慕就采用精钢或黄铜鞋跟为精致女鞋增添优雅色彩；因受已发掘的埃及法老杜唐卡蒙（Tutankhamen）的陵墓而激发的灵感，所创作的金字塔形多磨面高跟便是著名的典范。而上世纪50年代，金属鞋跟的风靡流行更是达到了空前的鼎盛。

1955年，萨尔瓦托勒·菲拉格慕递交了多项意义非凡的专利申请，例如以铝质薄层为衬里，色彩缤纷的金属质感鞋跟；或者中间镂空、轻盈纤巧又不失坚韧结实的"笼"形鞋跟；以及更具卓越独创性的多层鞋跟，上面缀满华丽的宝石，镀金或镀银的金属配饰，经过极为细致的手工雕琢呈现出花边般的装饰效果。

但是，菲拉格慕所创作的最卓越非凡的杰作莫过于他于1956年申请专利的金属鞋底。当时，他受一位澳大利亚石油大亨的夫人所托，设计创作了他有生以来所制作的最昂贵的鞋品——一双18K金凉鞋。为此，菲拉格慕携手佛罗伦萨的金匠工艺师在旧桥（Ponte Vecchio）倾力协作，金匠们制造出特制细链制成鞋帮，并将鞋底和鞋跟镀以黄金并配以龙的浮雕图案。这一奢华财富和卓绝工艺的标志，在随后的一些晚装鞋款中经常被"借鉴"，例如2005-2006年秋冬款系列中的Boreale凉鞋—将过去的令人过目难忘的旷世杰作转变为当代设计的元素。

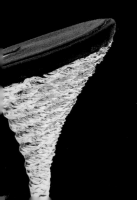

闪耀华丽的鞋跟和鞋底

Pull-over gold kid upper. High heel in layers of brass in decreasing sizes repeats the pyramid motif. 1930.

18kt gold sandal. 1956. Ferragamo created the most costly shoe he'd ever made for an Australian customer, wife of an oil magnate. It was realised in collaboration with the Florentine goldsmiths on the Ponte Vecchio.

Sandal with upper in black satin. High stiletto heel formed of brass cage. 1955.

Boreale sandal with upper in satin and heel in gilt metal. Fall/Winter 2005–6.

金黄色小山羊皮鞋帮的Pull-over凉鞋。高跟，呈铜质分层渐缩式结构，再现了金字塔的造型构思。1930年系列。

18K金凉鞋。1956年，菲拉格慕为一位澳大利亚顾客，一名石油大亨的夫人创作的他毕生最昂贵的鞋履。其制作由他与佛罗伦萨的金匠工艺师在旧桥共同完成。

黑色绸缎鞋帮凉鞋。尖头高跟，呈铜质笼形结构。1955年系列。

"Boreale"凉鞋，绸缎鞋帮，镀金金属鞋跟。2005-2006年秋冬系列。

Glam collection, *Strass* jewelled sandal. Cage heel with micron-geometric patterns studded with rhinestones. October 2006.

"Glam"系列中的"Strass"鞋款。镶嵌华丽宝石的凉鞋。笼形鞋跟配以精致几何图案，镶嵌晶莹闪耀的莱茵石。2006年10月系列。

精刻鞋跟

Creativity in heels was carried forward by Fiamma Ferragamo, who produced a number of famous sculpted heel patents which won her the Neiman Marcus Award in 1967, twenty years after her father had won it.

菲安玛·菲拉格慕继承父业，不断创新，推出了一系列著名的专利雕刻鞋跟。这些非凡的作品于1967年，在其父荣获尼曼·马库斯（Neiman Marcus）大奖的20年之后，又为她赢得了这一殊荣。

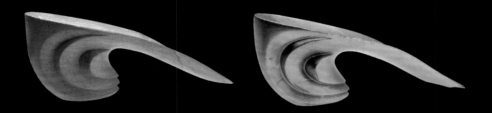

Sculpted heels, patented by Fiamma Ferragamo in 1966–67.

一精雕鞋跟，菲安玛·菲拉格慕1966-67年专利作品。

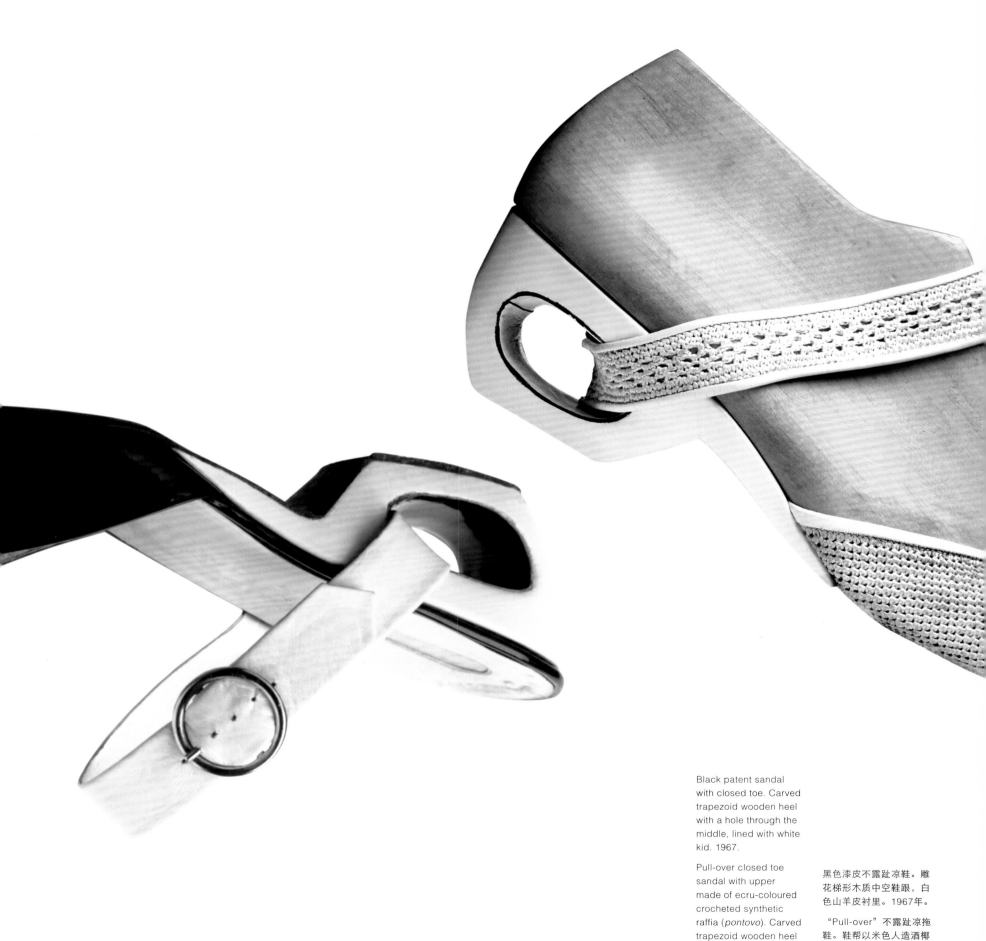

Black patent sandal with closed toe. Carved trapezoid wooden heel with a hole through the middle, lined with white kid. 1967.

Pull-over closed toe sandal with upper made of ecru-coloured crocheted synthetic raffia (*pontovo*). Carved trapezoid wooden heel with a hole through the middle, lined with white calf. 1968.

黑色漆皮不露趾凉鞋。雕花梯形木质中空鞋跟，白色山羊皮衬里。1967年。

"Pull-over"不露趾凉拖鞋。鞋帮以米色人造酒椰纤维钩织而成雕花梯形木质中空鞋跟，白色小牛皮衬里。1968年。

Kimo 女鞋

In 1951 Ferragamo patented a new kind of woman's shoe. Underneath it revealed a close fitting sock in a variety of colours and materials, called a *Kimo* and inspired by the Japanese *tabi*. This model was used by Ferragamo for the first ever Italian fashion show, featuring clothes by Schuberth, which took place in Florence, at the home of Giovanbattista Giorgini, on 12 February 1951. The concept of a multi-purpose model has been used by Ferragamo several times over the years in his creation of accessories, from bags to eyewear.

1951年，菲拉格慕为一款全新女鞋申请了专利。此款鞋品同时启发了与其配套穿着的短袜的诞生，称为"Kimo"，采用多种多样的颜色和质地制成，设计灵感来源于日本的厚底短袜。同年2月12日，菲拉格慕选用这一鞋款参加了在佛罗伦萨时装商人乔万·巴蒂斯塔·吉奥吉尼（Giovanbattista Giorgini）家中举行的，以舒伯特（Schuberth）的时装作品为主题的首届意大利时装展。在随后的岁月里，菲拉格慕曾多次将这一多功能款式的创意应用于从皮包到时尚眼镜等各种配件的创作中。

Invention patent 472261, 13 June 1952. Ladies' sandal combined with a counter-shoe sticking to the foot.

发明专利第472261号，1952年6月13日。女式凉鞋，内带合脚软质鞋。

Sandal with upper in black satin. Black satin stocking, called a *Kimo*. Also in gold kid and red satin. 1951

Capri group. Black patent leather bucket bag with removable liner in terry-cloth. Spring/ Summer 1996.

黑色绸缎鞋帮凉鞋。名为 "Kimo" 的黑色绸缎短袜。另外还有金黄色小山羊皮和红色绸缎质地的款式。1951年系列。

"Capri" 系列。黑色优雅皮质桶形提包，带可拆卸绒布衬里。1996年春夏系列。

Sunglasses with flexible non-warping metal frames and featuring rings in different colours that can be changed at will. 2001.

太阳镜，搭配Asta flex抗变形金属镜架，镜框采用多种颜色，可随意选配。2001年系列。

Patchwork

The use of patchwork has been one of the most recurrent themes in Salvatore Ferragamo footwear since the very beginning. It became one of its stylistic hallmarks, over and above the vicissitudes of fashion and tastes, the perfect expression of Ferragamo's predilection for combining colours and materials and renewing the language of fashion even when using the most traditional of leathers. The originality of his work should be seen in the context of the early twentieth century, in which acceptance of unusual materials and surprising colour combinations signalled changing attitudes to clothing and accessories.

It was in this climate that Sonia Delaunay, wife of the painter Robert and a key influence in figurative art and the applied arts, was developing new decorative solutions in her "simultaneous" clothes, fabrics and patchwork. The inspiration behind patchwork wasn't only, however, an expression of new artistic trends – it was also a remarkable interest in the tradition of hand-made quilts, the classic fabrics made of different materials sewn together as in North America, where Ferragamo did his apprenticeship.

The first patchwork uppers by Ferragamo appeared in the 1920s. These creations, cross- or tent-stitched with silk or cotton thread, in which calfskin alternated with rectangles of crocodile and suede, ton sur ton, or variously coloured suedes in geometrical arrangements, are striking examples of how Ferragamo changed an entire idiom using the most traditional of skins. In fact, they became a leitmotiv in subsequent collections, even after Salvatore's death in 1960. They were adapted in the clothing as well as the footwear and in all the leather accessories.

拼接工艺

从萨尔瓦托勒·菲拉格慕制作鞋履的初期至今，拼接工艺一直是他最常使用的主题之一。任凭潮流与品味更替变迁，拼接工艺始终诠释着菲拉格慕对缤纷的色彩和迥异的材质相互完美结合的青睐，以及他对使用最传统的皮革重新定义时尚语言的热衷，从而使其成为了菲拉格慕标志性的风格之一。二十世纪初，独特材质和艳丽色彩的风靡，宣告着人们对时装、配饰审美的转变，菲拉格慕创新的拼接工艺正是在这样的时代背景下应运而生。

受这一氛围的影响，著名画家罗伯特·德劳内（Robert Delaunay）的妻子、形象艺术与实用艺术领域极具影响力的艺术家索尼亚·德劳内（Sonia Delaunay），也在她"同时期"设计创作的服装、布料以及拼接作品中探索着全新的装饰风格。然而，拼接工艺所蕴含的灵感，不仅是一种全新艺术潮流的展示，还植根于人们对手工缝纫传统的浓厚兴趣，正如北美地区盛行的由多种不同材质混合缝制而成的经典面料，菲拉格慕在北美做学徒时就深受感染。

菲拉格慕创作的第一批拼接鞋履诞生于上世纪二十年代。他将小牛皮与颜色相仿的长方形鳄鱼皮、绒面革等材料，或者色彩缤纷的绒面革排列成几何图案，使用丝线或棉线以十字针法或斜向平行针法将它们拼接起来。它们是菲拉格慕采用最传统的皮革创造出的焕然一新风格的惊世杰作。事实上，这些作品成为随后作品系列反复沿用的主题，甚至萨尔瓦托勒于1960年逝世之后依然兴盛不衰，广泛应用于服装、鞋履以及各种皮质配件的设计创作中。

Shoe with suede upper in
a patchwork of coloured
squares. Four-layer cork
wedge heel lined with
suede. 1942.

Patchwork jacket in
"patchwork" suede.
Fall/Winter 1989–90.

鞋帮以多色方块绒面革拼
接而成的鞋款。四层软木
楔形鞋跟，内衬绒面革。
1942年系列。

"拼接"夹克，以"拼
接"绒面革制成。
1989-1990年秋冬系列。

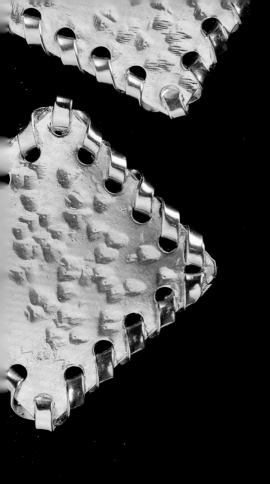

Patchwork group.
Gilt metal bracelet
and earrings.
Fall/Winter 1989–90.

Black suede evening bag
with a gilt metal frame
featuring the *Patchwork*
motif. Fall/Winter
1995–96.

"拼接"系列饰品。
镀金金属手镯和耳环。
1989-1990年秋冬系列。

黑色绒面革晚装女包，
配带"拼接"风格镀金金
属框架。1995-1996年秋
冬系列。

Bags, shoes and belts
in patchwork suede.
Fall/Winter 2000–1.

拼接绒面革包、鞋和腰
带。2000-2001年秋冬
系列。

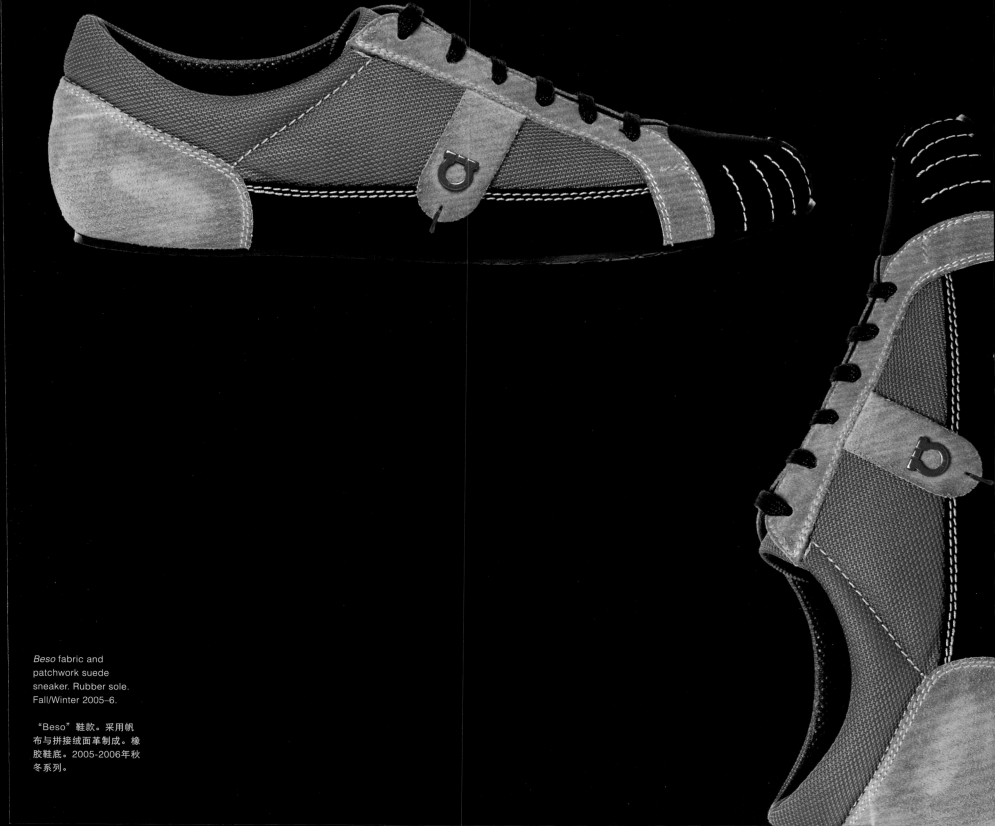

Beso fabric and
patchwork suede
sneaker. Rubber sole.
Fall/Winter 2005–6.

"Beso"鞋款。采用帆
布与拼接绒面革制成。橡
胶鞋底。2005-2006年秋
冬系列。

Game

女鞋

One of the models exemplifying Ferragamo's fertile imagination is a 1930 black kid pump with a Louis-XV-style heel and rounded toe, whose upper has a geometrical *Labyrinth* pattern (as it was defined in the patent), created in pearl-grey chain-stitching done with a mechanical needle (a leather embroidering process known in English as "tambour work").

This model with its geometrical decoration demonstrates Ferragamo's attention to the art of his times, especially Futurism and Cubism and collage and papier collé work pioneered by Pablo Picasso and Georges Braque.

The importance of this model as a symbol of Ferragamo's creativity and fashion-forward intuition made it the inspiration for an updated version and bag and shoe collection called *Game* in the Fall/Winter 2003–4. Subsequently, the pump became the subject or object on which nineteen contemporary artists could freely express their creativity, using various work techniques.

Game女鞋是体现菲拉格慕丰富想象力的经典杰作之一，这款诞生于1930年的黑色小山羊皮浅口高跟鞋采用路易十五风格的高跟和浑圆的鞋头，鞋帮饰有几何"迷宫"图案（已在其专利说明书中声明），用机械锈针以珍珠色链形刺绣法制作而成（一种在中文里被称之为"钩针编织"的皮革刺绣工艺）。

这一鞋款及其几何形饰纹是菲拉格慕向他所处时代杰出艺术的献礼，尤其是以帕布鲁·毕加索（Pablo Picasso）和乔治·布拉克（Georges Braque）为先驱的创新性未来派、立体派和拼贴艺术。

这一鞋款，作为菲拉格慕非凡创作力与敏锐的时尚走势直觉的典范，具有独一无二的重要意义。这使其成为了2003-2004年秋冬款系列中升级款以及称为"Game"的皮包和鞋品系列的灵感之源。鉴此，这也使19名当代艺术家得以以"Game"女鞋为主题或对象，自由地采用各种制作工艺尽情宣泄他们卓越超凡的创作才华。

1930

2003

Patent 7815, 28 January 1931. Ladies' elegant shoe with *Labyrinth* motif.

Pump with a dark grey kid upper embroidered in a *Labyrinth* design in chain-stitching done with a mechanical needle. Rounded toe. Wooden Louis XV heel, covered in embroidered kid, 1930.

High-heeled *Game* pump in black calf, embroidered in the *Labyrinth* design in ecru.

1931年1月28日取得专利，号码为7815。饰有迷宫图案的优雅女鞋。

深灰色小山羊皮浅口高跟鞋，鞋帮以链形机械绣花针绣有"迷宫"图案。圆形鞋头。路易十五风格木质鞋跟，外包刺绣小山羊皮。1930年。

黑色小牛皮制"Game"浅口高跟鞋，饰有白色"迷宫"图案。

Sunglasses with acetate frontal and lacquered metal temples, in which the 3-D play of full and hollow spaces reproduces the optical *Labyrinth* effect of the original design.

Gant high-top boot, in black calf, embroidered in the *Labyrinth* design in ecru.

Double-strap shoulder bag with black methacrylate frame and double *Gancino* claps in metal. Soft black calf leather embroidered in the *Labyrinth* design in ecru.

太阳镜，采用乙酸酯镜片和涂漆金属镜架，其中的三维全空立体空间生动演绎了原始设计的光学"迷宫"效果。

"Gant"高筒皮靴，黑色小牛皮质地，饰有白色"迷宫"图案。

双肩带女式挎包，配带黑色树脂边框和双"Gancino"金属扣。柔软的黑色小牛皮质地，饰有白色"迷宫"图案。

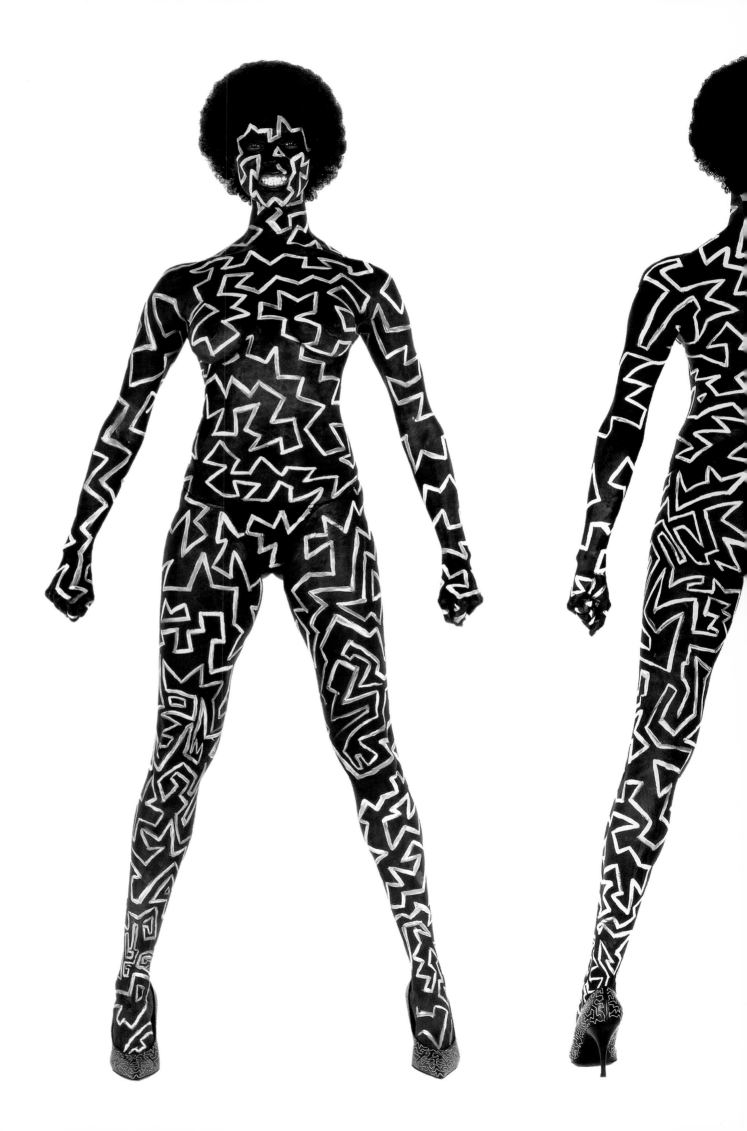

Vanessa Beecroft, *Keith*, 2003. Makeup Pierre Orlando, hair Franco Curletto. Digital prints, 35 x 25 inches each.

行为艺术家瓦妮莎·比克罗夫特、基思，2003年；化妆：皮埃尔·奥兰多，发型：佛朗哥·科莱托；数码印刷：每张35x25英寸。

The model is called *Salvatore*. This is the name that has been given to a double-handle "doctor's bag" with zippered side pockets which comes in three sizes and several colours and materials: heavy nylon and brushed black calf or black or brown pony skin with same-colour leather. The model is unique because of its construction. Its pocketed sides formed the double handle with a special convexity that gives the bag an anatomic grip.

The model is named for the company's founder, Salvatore Ferragamo and its shape was inspired by the big, burnt sienna pony skin and leather bag that Salvatore used from 1950 for work and especially for travel. It held the prototypes of his footwear and the tools of his craft. Thus it was the first bag to bear the Ferragamo signature, heralding the development of this product category beginning in the mid-1960s.

这一名为"萨尔瓦托勒"的款型，是一种带拉链侧袋的双拎手箱包，共有三种不同尺寸，采用多种颜色和材质制作，如厚尼龙搭配黑色拉绒小牛皮，或者黑色或棕色小马皮搭配相同色泽的其他皮革。它的构造别具匠心：侧面附带的口袋向上伸展构成提手，形成优美别致的凸面，赋予皮包独特的立体感。

这款皮包得名于企业创始人萨尔瓦托勒·菲拉格慕先生，而其造型的设计灵感则源自菲拉格慕先生1950年起在工作，特别是旅行中经常使用的一款由鲜赭褐色小马皮和其他皮革制成的大皮包。该包用来盛放菲拉格慕的鞋模和制鞋工具，因此是第一款承载着菲拉格慕独特风格的包款，预言着菲拉格慕箱包类产品自二十世纪60年代起的兴盛与发展。

The calf and pony skin bag that Salvatore Ferragamo used to carry his tools. 1950.

萨尔瓦托勒·菲拉格慕用于携带工具的皮包，由小牛皮和小马皮双面料制成。1950年。

"萨尔瓦托勒"皮包

Small double handle
Boston bag in grey
astrakhan and black calf.
Fall/Winter 2003–4.

精巧的双提手女士箱包，
采用灰色阿斯特拉罕羔
皮和黑色小牛皮双面料
制成。2003-2004年秋冬
系列。

标志

Before Salvatore Ferragamo arrived back in Italy in 1927, there was no Ferragamo logo. The footwear created by Salvatore almost exclusively for the movie industry was sold in his Hollywood Boot Shop. The name of Ferragamo stood for the man, the creative personality, but was not yet a brand.

It was with the setting up of the Ferragamo company in Florence that the first logo-type was devised: "Ferragamo's Creations Florence Italy". The name of the maker was tied to that of the city of Florence, explicitly suggesting that shoes crafted in a city of art were almost works of art themselves, collector's pieces.

Salvatore used his "Ferragamo's Creations Florence Italy" trademark to label his footwear, especially the evening models and the lined shoes made of top quality materials. With the extraordinary imagination that was peculiar to him and that he used not only to design shoes but also in his ante litteram marketing activities, he registered a number of trademarks including, for example, *Pompeian* for fabric or raffia summer shoes and *Leonardo by Ferragamo* for the *Capri* sandals in the 1950s.

The trademark that's known worldwide as the Ferragamo logo didn't come into being till after Salvatore Ferragamo's death in the 1960s. The family wanted the new trademark to feature the name of the departed founder, in the graphically recreated form of his original signature. Since then, this logo has labelled not only products and stores but also packaging and advertising campaigns. The initial F, for Ferragamo, also suggested a number of fabric patterns and even the name of a fragrance.

1927年萨尔瓦托勒·菲拉格慕重返意大利之前，尚没有菲拉格慕标志。那时，菲拉格慕几乎专门为电影业设计创作鞋品，并在自己位于好莱坞的靴店中出售。"菲拉格慕"这个名字代表着他个人，彰显着创新的个性，但还不是一种品牌。

直到公司在佛罗伦萨成立时，菲拉格慕才有了首个精心设计的标志："Ferragamo's Creations Florence Italy"（菲拉格慕创意，源自意大利佛罗伦萨）。它将鞋品的制作者与佛罗伦萨这个城市联系在一起，有着鲜明的寓意：创作于艺术之都的鞋品本身也是艺术杰作，是收藏家的珍品。

从那时起，菲拉格慕便使用"Ferragamo's Creations Florence Italy"作为标示自己鞋履的标志，尤其是晚装鞋款和采用顶级材质制作的加衬鞋款。菲拉格慕有着独到的想象力，这不仅在鞋品设计中彰显无遗，而且在营销活动中也大放异彩，鉴此，他先后注册了数个商标，其中包括为布质面料和酒椰纤维夏装鞋款注册的"Pompeian"和为50年代的卡普里凉鞋注册的"Leonardo by Ferragamo"商标。

然而，作为菲拉格慕品牌标志在世界上广为人知的商标却是在萨尔瓦托勒·菲拉格慕于60年代去世之后才诞生的。当时，家族希望以离世的品牌创始人的名字设计一款全新的商标，于是便在他原始签名的基础上加以修饰而成。从那时起，这个标志不仅成了菲拉格慕产品和专卖店的标识，而且还出现在产品包装及广告宣传活动中。同时，菲拉格慕（Ferragamo）姓氏的首字母"F"也成为品牌丰富的织物图案，甚至还是一款香水的名字。

The 1987–88 advertising
campaign was based on
the Salvatore Ferragamo
logo and the company's
headquarters in Palazzo
Spini Feroni.

以萨尔瓦托勒·菲拉格慕
标志和位于费罗尼—斯皮
尼大宅（Palazzo Spini
Feroni）的公司总部为主
题的1987-1988年广告宣
传活动。

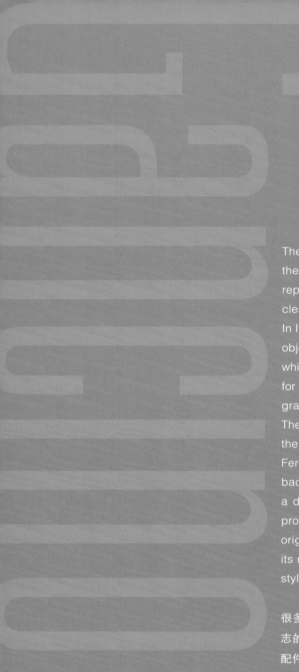

Gancino

The *Gancino* is the first thing that comes to the minds of many whenever they hear the Ferragamo name. This distinctive symbol is more than just that; it has come to represent the brand, appearing on a multitude of Ferragamo accessories and articles of clothing.

In Italian, the word *gancino* denotes a small metal clasp used to hang or hook various objects. This is how the *Gancino* began to be used in the 1970s as the clasp for a bag, which Fiamma, the eldest of Wanda and Salvatore Ferragamo's six children, created for her mother. However, an article in the German press dated 1958 shows a photograph of a bag designed by Salvatore Ferragamo with a very similar adornment.

The origin of the *Gancino* remains a mystery. Within the company, legend has it that the source of inspiration for its design was the wrought-iron gate to Palazzo Spini Feroni, the building that houses the Ferragamo business in Florence and dates back to Medieval times. More likely, the idea came about in the 1950s for use as a distinctive symbol, when the development of Made in Italy products led to the proliferation of symbols and trademarks of all shapes and sizes. Regardless of its origin, the *Gancino* was increasingly used in leather accessories and shoes until its rise to fame in the 1980s – its success residing in the elegant balance between style and function.

很多人听到菲拉格慕的名字时，首先浮现在脑海中的就是"Gancino"。这一独特标志的意义已经远超出其本身；它已是这一伟大品牌的代名词，频频呈现于菲拉格慕的配件和服装作品上。

标志

在意大利语中，"Gancino"一词指用于悬挂或钩钓各种物品的小金属扣。上世纪七十年代，蔓达和萨尔瓦托勒·菲拉格慕夫妇的六个子女中的长女菲安玛在为母亲设计皮包时，首次采用了"Gancino"作为卡扣。然而，早在1958年，在一份德国报纸上刊登的一幅萨尔瓦托勒·菲拉格慕先生设计的一款皮包的照片中就带有极为相似的饰件。

"Gancino"的起源至今仍充满了神秘。公司内部流传的说法是该设计的灵感源自费罗尼—斯皮尼大宅（Palazzo Spini Feroni）的锻铁大门，这座中世纪的古堡是菲拉格慕公司位于佛罗伦萨的总部。但更可能的情形是：这一创意，作为一种独特的标志，诞生于上世纪五十年代；当时"意大利制造"产品的蓬勃发展，致使各种形状和大小的标志、商标纷纷涌现。无论起源如何，"Gancino"已被越来越多地应用于菲拉格慕的各种皮革配件和鞋品中，在上世纪八十年代声名远扬，逐渐在优雅风格和实用功能之间取得了完美平衡。

Gancini group. Soft brown brushed calfskin rigid double handle large handbag. Double fastener with *Gancino* ornaments in golden metal. Spring/Summer 1997.

"Gancini系列"。大号手提包，选用柔软的棕色拉绒小牛皮制成，硬质双提手。双卡扣，饰有金黄色"Gancini"金属饰件。1997年春夏系列。

1995

1996—97

1999

1996

1997

2000

1992—93

1997

1997—98

1995

1999—2000

2001

Gancini group.
The classic Ferragamo
bag, with a handle and
a *Gancino* fastening,
is made of different
materials every season,
from rubber to Plexiglas,
from wicker to metal,
from wood to plaited
calfskin or the more
classic crocodile.

"Gancini系列"。菲拉
格慕经典款皮包，带提手
和"Gancino"饰扣。该
系列皮包选用的材质随季
度的不同而不同，从橡胶
到树脂玻璃，从柳条到金
属，从木材到编织小牛皮
或更为经典的鳄鱼皮革。

Gancini group. Large coloured crocodile bag with two rigid handles. Double fastening with gilt *Gancino* patterned metal accessories. The model was created by Fiamma Ferragamo for her mother. Fall/Winter 1988–89.

"Gancini系列"。大号彩色鳄鱼皮皮包，带两个硬质提手。双镀金卡扣，带"Gancini"图案金属配件。该款皮包由菲安玛·菲拉格慕女士为其母亲设计创作。1988-1989年秋冬系列。

Gancini group. Versatile handbags with nickel signature hardware, plastic handles, removable shoulder strap and interchangeable pouches. Patent leather or fabric print. Fall/Winter 1996–97.

"Gancini 系列"。多功能手提包，饰有镍金属标志，塑料提手、可拆式肩带以及可调换的内袋：漆皮或印花布面。1996-1997年秋冬系列。

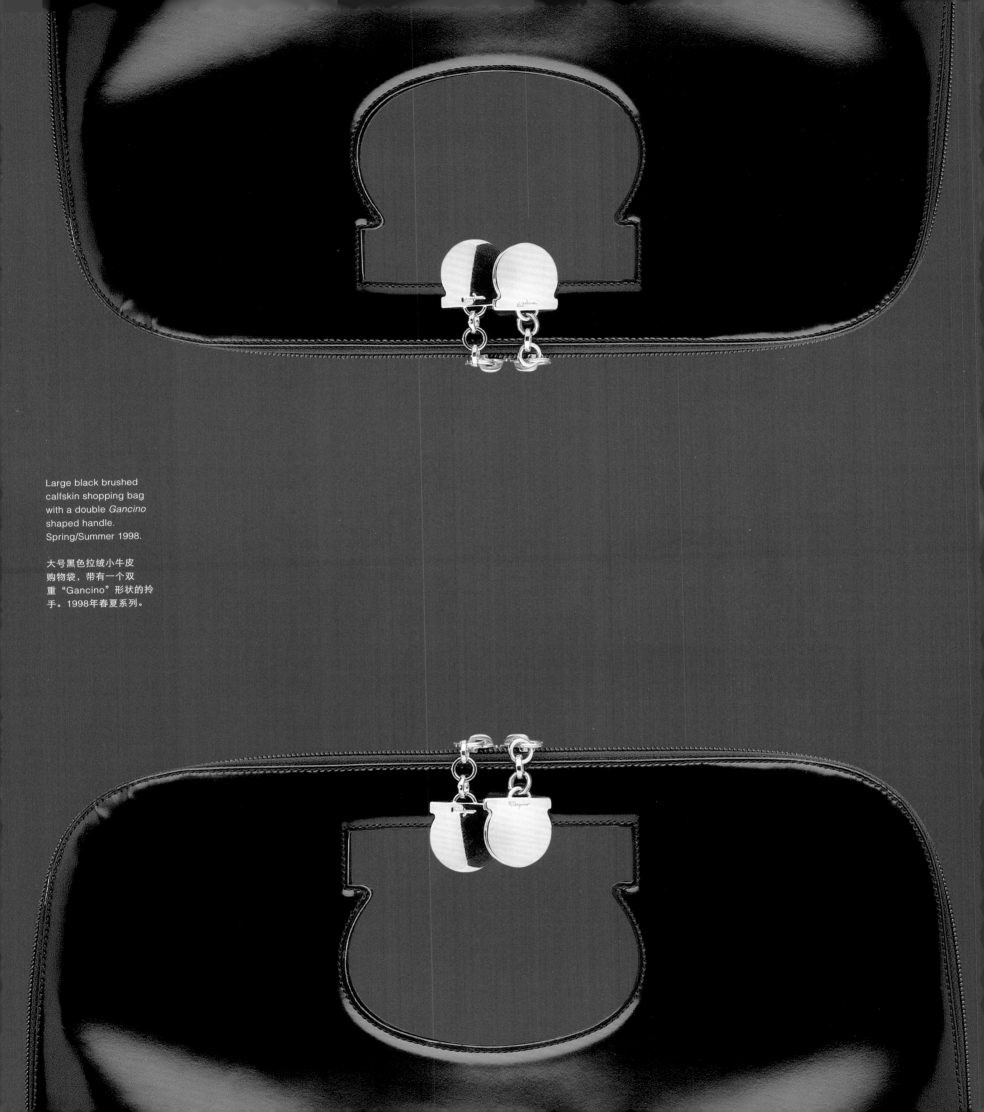

Large black brushed
calfskin shopping bag
with a double *Gancino*
shaped handle.
Spring/Summer 1998.

大号黑色拉绒小牛皮
购物袋，带有一个双
重"Gancino"形状的拎
手。1998年春夏系列。

The *Gancino* emblem also became a logo printed on fabrics for use in bags, clothing and silk scarves. Fall/Winter 2000–1.

"Gancino" 标志也被制作成印花图案，压制到包、服装和丝巾等的面料上。2000-2001年秋冬系列。

"Gancini系列"。小号
驼色小牛皮皮包,带镀金
手镯形金属提手。1995-
1996年秋冬系列。

"Gancini系列"。仿古
硬质山羊皮提手皮包。
1995-1996年秋冬系列。

Gancini group. Small
camel calfskin bag
with a gilt metal
bracelet-style handle.
Fall/Winter 1995–96.

Gancini group. Bag
with a rigid, antique
gilt finish suede handle.
Fall/Winter 1995–96.

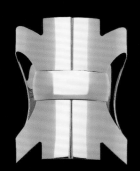

Gancini group.
Gold logo bracelets.
Fall/Winter 1992–93.

Gancini group. Gold
logo chain evening bag.
Spring/Summer 2001.

"Gancini系列"。徽标
志图案的金属质手镯。
1992-1993年秋冬系列。

"Gancini系列"。晚装皮
包，带有标志图案的黄金
链带。2001年春夏系列。

Gancini group. Gancino
chain belt with purse.
Spring/Summer 1994
and Fall/Winter 1995–96.

"Gancini系列"。
"Gancino"链带，配
有皮夹。1994年春夏和
1995-1996年秋冬系列。

Tasha model. Moccasins with *Gancino* motifs. Spring/Summer 1994 and Fall/Winter 1993–94.

Tasha model. Moccasin made of antique gilt, cotter, Sheffield finish nappa with *Gancino* motifs. Fall/Winter 1995–96.

"Tasha" 款皮鞋。饰有 "Gancino" 图案。1994年春夏和1993-1994年秋冬系列。

"Tasha" 款皮鞋。软质鹿皮质地，采用经过谢菲尔德处理的仿古金色软羊革制成，饰有 "Gancino" 标志的锁销。1995-1996年秋冬系列。

女鞋

Vara started life in 1978, a creation of Fiamma Ferragamo, Wanda and Salvatore Ferragamo's eldest daughter. "When it came out", said Fiamma in an interview, "the boutique line didn't have a model that was both sporty and elegant. The designers set to work on a shape that had been tried and tested for some seasons and was well known to be comfortable, with a low heel and round toe. The prototype was given a small oval decoration and a bow improvised out of a strip of grosgrain from the atelier. It seemed a good idea and we decided to pass the shoe on to a modeller, asking him to make a bow in the same leather as the uppers. In actual fact, the message was misunderstood and the bow stayed in grosgrains."

Since then, production of the Vara has never stopped, and more than a million pairs have been sold, making it the most successful shoe in its category.

The Vara's success lies in its elegantly minimalist design – a closed, round-toe shoe with a low heel, grosgrain bow and gold plaque bearing the Ferragamo logo. Its sophisticated style has left a mark on Ferragamo clothing and all of its accessories, from buttons and belts to jewellery and bags. Over the years, it has been made in every possible colour, fabric and skin, without losing any of its charm. It has inspired countless imitations.

The most recent version, the Varina, is offered in the Spring 2008 collection, and puts a modern spin on this Ferragamo classic. Updating the Vara's soft lines into a ballerina style, the Varina has kept the gold plaque and fabric bow, along with a grosgrain ribbon stitched along the trim.

Vara女鞋诞生于1978年，由萨尔瓦托勒与蔓达·菲拉格慕夫妇的长女菲安玛设计创作。菲安玛在一次采访中回忆道："Vara女鞋面世之前，我们的精品系列中还没有运动气息与优雅风格兼备的鞋款。于是设计师们开始倾力打造这样的鞋款，经过多个季节的反复尝试和测试，终于推出舒适性无人不晓的矮跟、圆头款Vara女鞋。出自工作室的设计原型上带有小巧的椭圆形缀饰和罗缎丝带随意盘起的蝴蝶结。这似乎是个好主意，于是我们决定将原型交给制模师，请他采用与鞋帮相同的皮革制作蝴蝶结。但事实上，制模师误会了我们的本意，保留了罗缎蝴蝶结。"

自那时起，Vara女鞋的生产从未停止过，至今已销售了百万双以上，这因而也使其成为了同类鞋品中最风靡的款式。Vara女鞋的成功在于其优雅的简约式设计—浑圆的鞋头、低矮的鞋跟、罗缎蝴蝶结以及刻有菲拉格慕标识的金属饰牌。它的精致华美的风格对菲拉格慕时装，乃至钮扣、腰带、珠宝和皮包等饰件都打上了深深的烙印。多年来，Vara女鞋的制作采用过各种各样的颜色、面料和皮革，款款都不失迷人的魅力。鉴此，受其启发的升级款不计其数。最近的一款是2008年春季款系列中的Varina女鞋，它为菲拉格慕的经典系列赋予了现代精髓。在将Vara女鞋柔和的线条提升为芭蕾舞鞋风格的同时，Varina女鞋保留了金属饰牌和罗缎蝴蝶结以及罗缎丝带镶边。

Wide red grosgrain belt
with signature *Vara* bow.
Spring/Summer 1988.

宽型红色罗缎腰带，
饰有"Vara"蝴蝶结。
1988年春夏系列。

Vara red patent shoulder
bag with *Vara* bow.
Spring/Summer 1989.
(In black patent,
Fall/Winter 1996–97).

Vara, a shoe created in
1978 and remade every
year in different colours
and materials.

"Vara" 系列。饰
有"Vara"蝴蝶结的女
式挎包。红色漆皮款，
1989年春夏系列。黑色
漆皮款，1996-1997年秋
冬系列。

"Vara"女鞋。原创于
1978年，其后每年都以
不同的色彩和材质推出
新款。

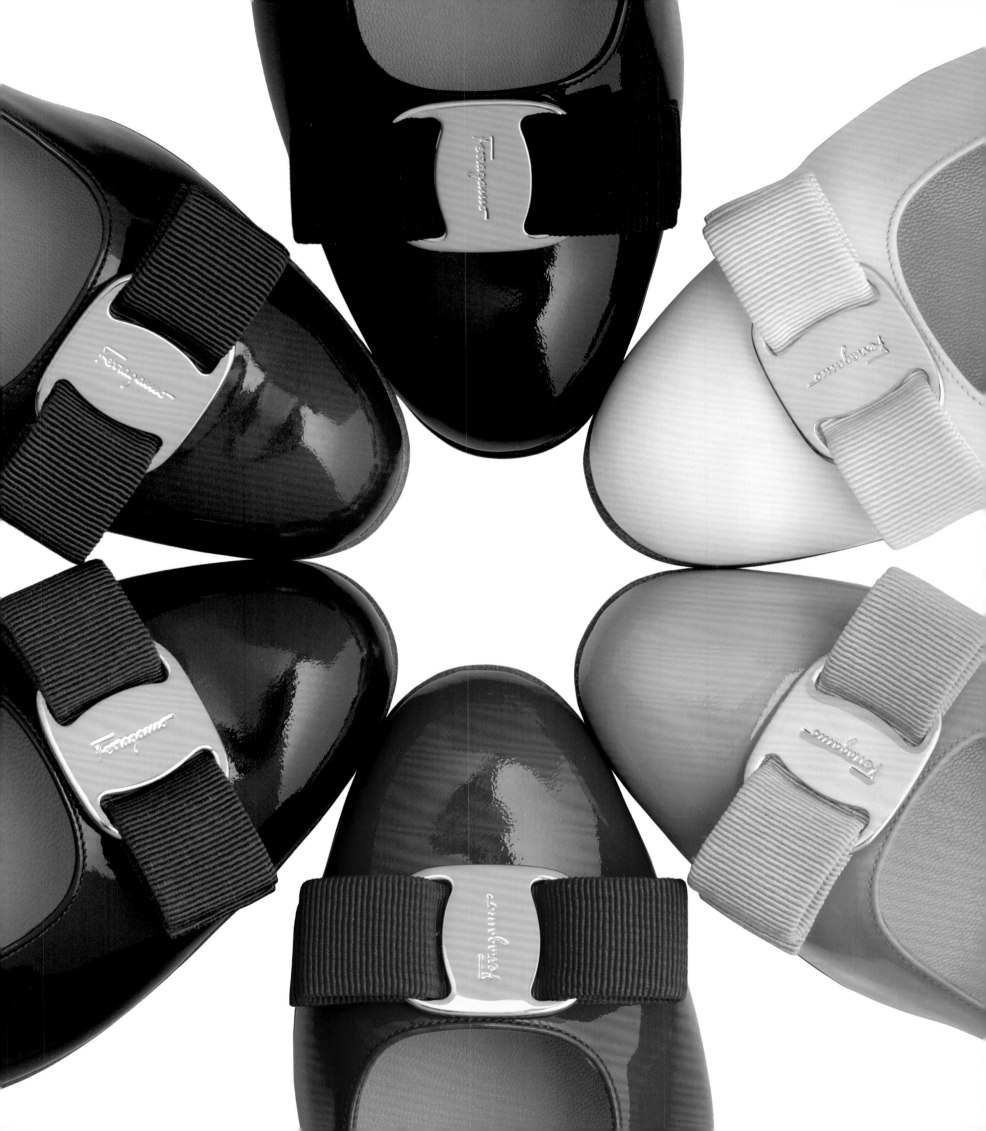

Suit in black suede
with decoration in black
grosgrain with *Vara* bow.
Fall/Winter 1990–91.

黑色绒面革套装，饰有
黑色罗缎和"Vara"蝴
蝶结。1990-1991年秋冬
系列。

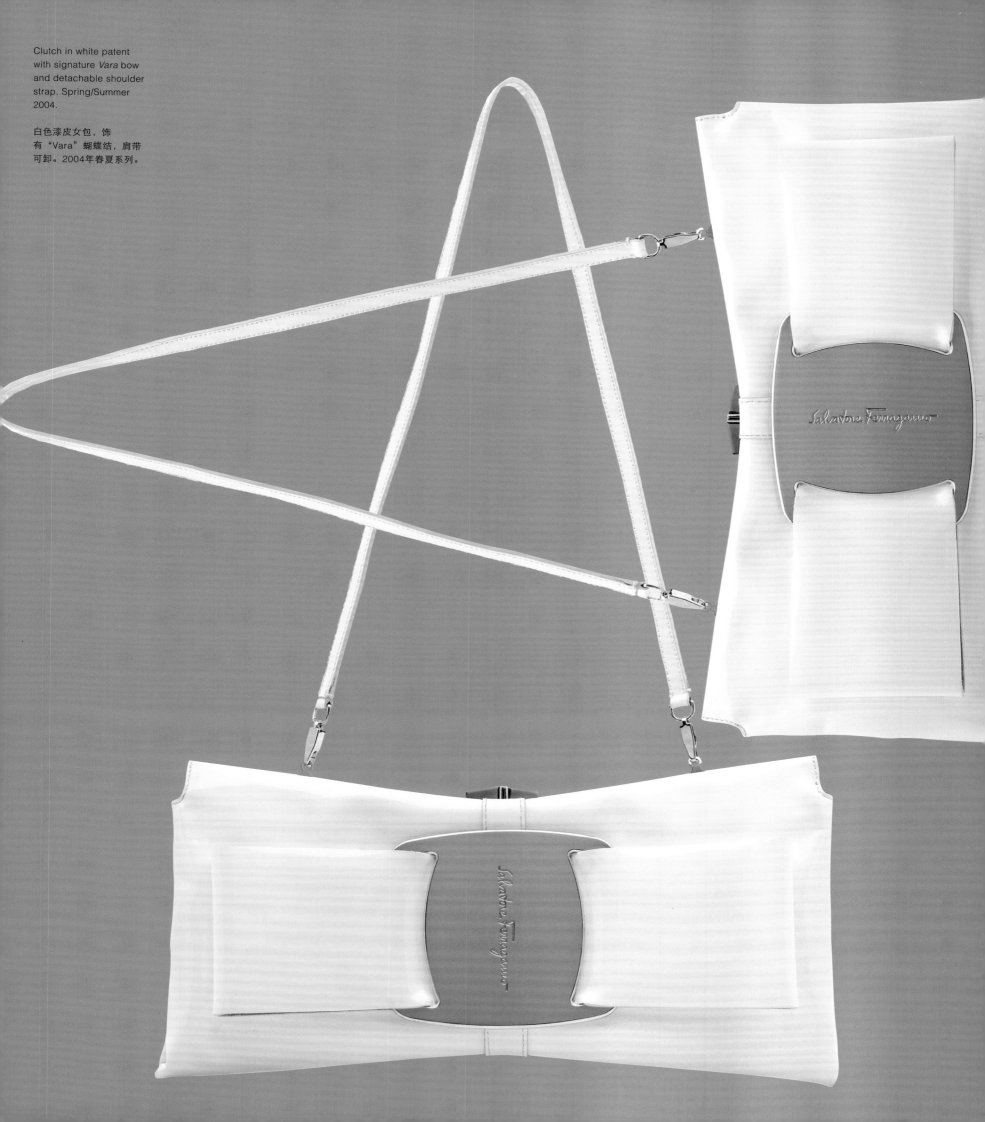

Clutch in white patent
with signature *Vara* bow
and detachable shoulder
strap. Spring/Summer
2004.

白色漆皮女包，饰
有"Vara"蝴蝶结，肩带
可卸。2004年春夏系列。

The new *Varina*, the
latest *Vara*-inspired
ballerina. Spring/Summer
2008.

全新"Varina"女鞋：
受"Vara"灵感激发而创
作的最新芭蕾舞鞋风格的
女式鞋款。2008年春夏
系列。

The decorative
grosgrain bow with a
metal Ferragamo logo.

饰有金属菲拉格慕标识的
装饰性罗缎蝴蝶结。

Shoes

设计

In 1985 a retrospective exhibition of the history of Salvatore Ferragamo was held in Palazzo Strozzi, Florence. It was the first time in Italy that the products of a fashion company still in business – footwear in this case – had been presented as works of twentieth-century art and design. After Palazzo Strozzi, the exhibition was shown in a number of other museums, and the over 10,000 Ferragamo footwear models, dating back as far as 1920 and conserved in Ferragamo's Florence headquarters (Palazzo Spini Feroni), became the core of the Salvatore Ferragamo Museum, dedicated to the history of the founder. Over this long period, Ferragamo stylists have often drawn inspiration from the museum when working on their collections. The designers of silk scarves in particular created a series of graphic motifs based on famous Ferragamo shoes. The first of these designs was called *Shoes*, a theme then used to create bijoux, clothing fabrics, bag fastenings, buttons and footwear decorations, thus becoming a decorative motif unique in the world of fashion design, an original hallmark of the Ferragamo brand.

1985年，"萨尔瓦托勒·菲拉格慕历史回顾展"在佛罗伦萨的斯特罗兹宫（Palazzo Strozzi）隆重开幕。这是意大利历史上仍在运营中的时装公司首次将产品—鞋类制品—作为20世纪的艺术设计品面向大众展出。自在斯特罗兹宫（Palazzo Strozzi）举办此次展览之后，菲拉格慕鞋履又相继移师其他多家博物馆展出。鉴此，公司位于佛罗伦萨的总部费罗尼—斯皮尼大宅（Palazzo Spini Feroni）中珍藏着一万多款菲拉格慕经典鞋品，其历史最早可追溯到1920年，因此而成为了萨尔瓦托勒·菲拉格慕博物馆的精髓，见证着品牌创始人的辉煌历史。多年来，菲拉格慕的设计师们经常从这些馆藏品中汲取创作灵感。特别值得一提的是，丝巾设计师们寻源于著名的菲拉格慕鞋品，设计并创作了一系列精美绝伦的图案。其中首款这样的设计是被称为"Shoes"的图案，该主题随即被广泛地用于珠宝、服装面料、包卡扣、纽扣和鞋品的装饰中，因此成为了时装设计领域独具一格的装饰图案，同时也是菲拉格慕品牌独树一帜的标志性图案。

Belt in gilt metal with Salvatore Ferragamo Museum shoe motif. Spring/Summer 1991.

镀金金属腰带，饰有萨尔瓦托勒·菲拉格慕博物馆藏鞋品图案。1991年春夏系列。

Shoes scarf, 90 x 90 cm.
Silk twill. Spring/Summer
1989.

"Shoes" 丝巾（90 x 90
厘米），真丝斜纹绸。
1989年春夏系列。

Stretch fabric track
suit with a shoe model
pattern printed on it.
Spring/Summer 1991.

弹性面料径赛服，饰有印
花精美鞋品图案。1991年
春夏系列。

Advertising campaign.
Fall/Winter 1990–91.

广告促销活动。
1990-1991年秋冬系列。

"It often happens that I leap ahead, and many times I have been successful in breaking with the current fashion trend and making the new styles immediately popular." (from *Shoemaker of Dreams. The Autobiography of Salvatore Ferragamo*)

"我往往因而领风气之先，有好几次甚至成功突破当前的时尚潮流，让我的新设计马上风行起来。"（摘自萨尔瓦托勒·菲拉格慕的《梦鞋匠》）

Nature | 天然

Ferragamo is one of the Italian fashion houses whose silk accessories are one of its most powerful emblems. Its first silk scarves were made at the end of the 1950s by external designers, some of whom artists in their own right. The themes of choice were animals and famous monuments in various Italian cities. In the 1970s, ties were added on to the range, which was then extended to bags and clothing made using the same fabric and patterns as the scarves: a must for lovers of Ferragamo fashion. No less than the silk itself, the patterns that were printed on it became a hallmark of the Ferragamo style. Ethnic and even erudite motifs, often in the style of miniatures and illuminations in antique manuscripts and other decorative art forms, were preferred in the ties, while Nature prevailed in the *foulards*: flowers and the animal world, especially exotic species living in jungles and the savannah.

In the beginning the two decorative styles coincided. The first designs in the 1970s featured animals made with a floral patchwork technique that made even the most ferocious panthers look somehow domesticated. Subsequently, a different ferocity emerged in an endless stream of other powerfully creative patterns and motifs.

Over a month's work by many people is needed to produce a new Ferragamo silk scarf or tie. The end result is the fruit of an extraordinary collaboration between intuitive creativity and consummate industrial craft.

菲拉格慕是一家著名的意大利时装公司，其丰富的丝绸配件是该品牌最卓著的标志性产品之一。上世纪50年代末，菲拉格慕推出了首批丝巾产品，其设计由外部设计师创作，其中一些设计师采用了自己的艺术理念。所选主题是各种动物和意大利众多城市中远近闻名的纪念碑。70年代，系列中新增了多款领带，随后又拓展至使用相同面料与图案的箱包和服装：成为菲拉格慕时尚喜爱者的必备之物。

与丝巾本身的魅力相比，印制在上面的图案也毫不逊色，成为菲拉格慕风格的一大特色。民族风情以及更为复杂的装饰主题，通常以仿古手绘或其他装饰艺术形式的鲜亮彩绘或彩饰图案为特色，优先应用于领带系列；而丝巾系列盛行的则是花卉和动物王国等自然主题，尤其是栖身于丛林和草原，充满异国风情的奇珍异兽。

最初，丝巾的这两种装饰风格能相互融合，菲拉格慕70年代推出的首批设计便以拼缀技术将动物和花卉图案结合在一起，令即使是最凶猛的黑豹也显出几分温顺。随后，其他各种极具创意的图案和主题也源源不断地涌现出来，呈现出不同寻常的猛兽情态。

制作一款全新的菲拉格慕丝巾或领带需要许多人辛勤工作一个多月的时间，才能最终收获完美结合了才华横溢的创造力和极致精湛的行业技艺的累累硕果。

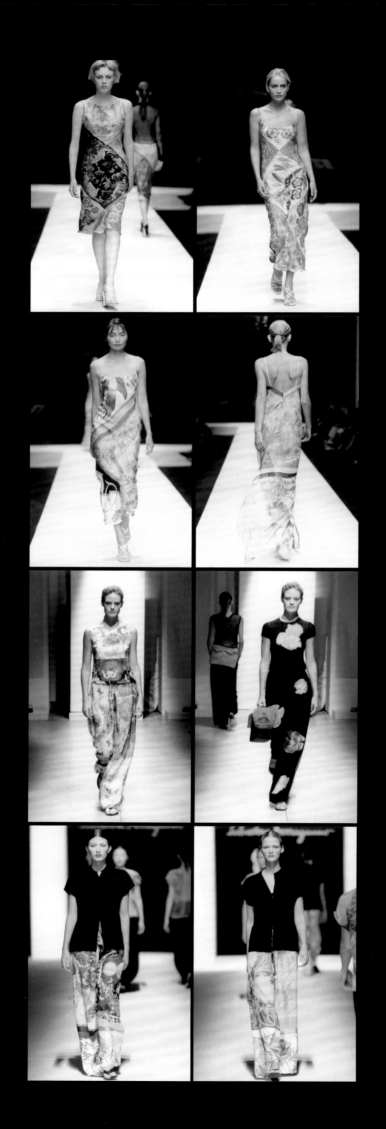

Spring/Summer 1998, 1999 and 2000 fashion shows with scarf dresses.

1998年、1999年和 2000年春夏丝绸围裙系列 时装展。

Spring/Summer
1987.

1987年春夏系列。

Shoe coated with a silk
twill scarf. Fall/Winter
1996–97.

Handbag coated
with a silk twill scarf.
Spring/Summer 1996.

外包斜纹丝巾的鞋履。
1996-1997年秋冬系列。

外包斜纹丝巾的手提包。
1996年春夏系列。

Fall/Winter 1996–97.

1996-1997年秋冬系列。

Fiera group. Shopping
handbag in printed
fabric. Spring/Summer
2007.

Pantera nera scarf.
90 x 90 cm silk twill.
Spring/Summer 1989.

"Fiera"系列。印花面
料手提购物包。2007年春
夏系列。

"Pantera nera"丝巾
（幅面90x90厘米），
斜纹丝绸面料。1989年春
夏系列。

"I have divided the women who have come to me into three categories: the Cinderella, the Venus and the Aristocrat. The Cinderella takes a shoe smaller than Size Six, the Venus takes Size Six, the Aristocract a Seven or larger." (from *Shoemaker of Dreams. The Autobiography of Salvatore Ferragamo*)

"我遇见过的女顾客可以分成三个类型——'灰姑娘'、'爱神'和'贵族'。'灰姑娘'穿小于6码的鞋，'爱神'穿刚好6码的鞋，'贵族'则穿7码或更大。"（摘自萨尔瓦托勒·菲拉格慕的《梦鞋匠》）

Cinema | 电影情缘

Salvatore Ferragamo and the Cinema: A Love Story. The career and successes of Salvatore Ferragamo, as of the company bearing his name, are a magnificent example of the relationship between fashion and cinema from 1920 on. When Salvatore moved to California, bringing with him his passion for shoes and exceptional craftsmanship, his first real work experience was with the movies. His first contract was with the American Film Company, who asked him to make boots for their westerns. Actors and actresses who wore Ferragamo shoes on set started getting made-to-measure shoes for themselves in the small shoe shop Ferragamo opened in Santa Barbara. Directors like Cecil B. De Mille, David W. Griffith, James Cruze and Raoul Walsh were the true source of his fortune. From Ferragamo they ordered shoes for films like *Way Down East* (D. W. Griffith, 1920), *The Ten Commandments* (C. B. De Mille, 1923), *The Covered Wagon* (J. Cruze, 1923) and *The Thief of Baghdad* (R. Walsh, 1924).

Cinema became then the fantastic generator of fashion and fashions that it is today. Ferragamo models soon became objects of desire and seduction and Salvatore earned the nickname "shoemaker to the stars". Famous actresses and actors like Pola Negri, Mary Pickford, Gloria Swanson, Joan Crawford, Rodolfo Valentino and Douglas Fairbanks jr were amongst his affectionate customers.

In 1923, on the wave of this success, Ferragamo was able to open the Hollywood Boot Shop on Hollywood Boulevard, on the corner of Las Palmas. It was a large and elegant store but with a discreet, cosy atmosphere. Many of the stars who filled the pages of American newspapers came to its opening or sent good luck cards and flowers.

Throughout the long years, the relationship with the cinema was never interrupted, continuing to provide highly important stimuli to Salvatore Ferragamo's creativity and to enhance the overall identity of his company.

In the 1950s, Palazzo Spini Feroni was already a must for celebrity actresses visiting Italy, such as Audrey Hepburn, Ava Gardner, Greta Garbo, Anna Magnani, Paulette Goddard, Lauren Bacall and Sophia Loren. Salvatore received them in person and was able to satisfy all their demands, however extravagant.

Film stars today carry on this loyalty to the name of Ferragamo. The difference being that what they want from the Ferragamo brand – shoes of course but also bags, clothes and accessories – they can find not only in Florence but in all the world's major cities.

Salvatore Ferragamo the company has retained the habit of working for big film productions, both by making accessories for them, such as the shoes worn by Mel Gibson in Wim Wenders' *The Million Dollar Hotel*, for example, or Jude Law's highly original carbon fibre overnight bag in Steven Spielberg's *AI*, and by working actively inside the production in close contact with costume designers. This happened in 1996, on Alan Parker's *Evita*, played by Madonna, in 1998 on Andy Tennant's *Ever After. A Cinderella Story* (with Drew Barrymore, Anjelica Huston and Jeanne Moreau) and more recently on Baz Luhrmann's *Australia*, with Nicole Kidman.

萨尔瓦托勒·菲拉格慕与电影：一个爱情传奇。 自公司以他的名字命名之日起，萨尔瓦托勒·菲拉格慕的职业生涯和成功事业便成为了上世纪20年代以来时尚界与电影界之间密切联系的完美典范。

当萨尔瓦托勒·菲拉格慕胸怀对制鞋的热情和精湛的技艺迁至加利福尼亚时，他的首次真正创作经历就是为电影制作鞋履：美国电影公司与他签下了第一份订单，请他为该公司的西部片制作皮靴。男女演员在片场穿过菲拉格慕鞋品后，很快便纷纷寻访他在圣芭芭拉（Santa Barbara）开的一家小鞋店，请菲拉格慕为自己量身制作鞋品。而像塞西尔·B·戴米尔（Cecil B. De Mille）、大卫·W·格利菲思（David W. Griffith）、詹姆士·克鲁兹（James Cruze）和拉乌尔·沃尔什（Raoul Walsh）等导演才是菲拉格慕真正的财富之源。他们为 《东方之路》（1920年D·W·格利菲思执导）、《十诫》（1923年C·B·戴米尔执导）、《篷车队》（1923年J·克鲁兹执导）和《巴格达大盗》(1924年R·沃尔什执导)等电影向菲拉格慕订购了大量鞋履。

电影成为了绝妙的时尚制造机，时至今日依然如此。菲拉格慕设计的鞋款很快便成为充满诱惑、令人痴迷的珍品，而菲拉格慕也因此赢得了"明星御用之鞋匠"这一美誉。如波拉·尼格丽（Pola Negri）、玛丽·碧克馥（Mary Pickford）、葛罗莉亚·史旺逊（Gloria Swanson）、琼·克劳馥（Joan Crawford）、鲁道夫·瓦伦蒂诺（Rodolfo Valentino）和道格拉斯·费尔班克斯（Douglas Fairbanks）等著名影星都是菲拉格慕忠实的顾客。1923年，借着这股成功的浪潮，菲拉格慕在好莱坞林荫大道的Las Palmas一角开办了"好莱坞鞋店"（Hollywood Boot Shop）。店面宽敞、高雅，弥漫着精致又舒适的氛围。鞋店举办开业典礼时，许多经常出现在美国大小报刊上的明星都前来祝贺，并送来了贺卡和鲜花。

多年以来，菲拉格慕与电影业的密切联系从未间断，这在提升菲拉格慕公司整体形象的同时，也一直是他重要的灵感源泉。

上世纪五十年代，费罗尼 – 斯皮尼大宅Palazzo Spini Feroni（菲拉格慕总部）已成为许多著名女星访问意大利时的必到之处，如奥黛丽·赫本（Audrey Hepburn）、艾娃·加德纳（Ava Gardner）、葛丽泰·嘉宝（Greta Garbo）、安娜·麦兰妮（Anna Magnani）、保利特·戈达德（Paulette Goddard）、劳伦·白考尔（Lauren Bacall）、索菲娅·罗兰（Sophia Loren）等影星都曾受到菲拉格慕的亲自接待。在那里，菲拉格慕能够满足她们的各种奇思妙想，无论这些想法如何奢华。

时至今日，电影明星们仍是菲拉格慕的忠实客户。只不过现在不仅在佛罗伦萨，而且在全世界各大城市中，他们都能找到自己心仪的菲拉格慕产品—无论是鞋品，还是服装、配件。

菲拉格慕公司始终保持着与各大电影公司密切合作的传统，不但为影片提供各种服饰，例如在维姆·文德斯（Wim Wenders）执导的《百万大饭店》中，梅尔·吉布森（Mel Gibson）穿的皮鞋以及在史蒂文·斯皮尔伯格（Steven Spielberg）执导的《人工智能》中，裘德·洛（Jude Law）携带的非凡创新的碳纤维旅行包，而且还与制作公司内部的化妆师们建立了密切的联系。这表现在1996年艾伦·帕克（Alan Parker）执导、麦当娜（Madonna）主演的影片《贝隆夫人》，在1998年安迪·塔南特（Andy Tennant）执导的影片《童话情真》（*Ever After*），演员包括德鲁·巴里摩尔（Drew Barrymore）、安洁莉卡·休斯顿（Anjelica Huston）和让娜·莫罗（Jeanne Moreau），以及近期巴兹·鲁赫曼（Baz Luhrmann）执导、妮可·基德曼（Nicole Kidman）主演的《澳大利亚》等多部电影中。

1. Joan Crawford in the Hollywood Boot Shop which Ferragamo opened in 1923.

2. Salvatore Ferragamo on Hollywood set.

1．琼·克劳馥（Joan Crawford）光顾菲拉格慕于1923年开办的"好莱坞鞋店"。

2．萨尔瓦托勒·菲拉格慕参观好莱坞片场。

3. Edna Cooper.

4. Lilian Gish in *Way Down East* by David Wark Griffith. 1920.

5, 6, 7. Two models created by Ferragamo for Mary Pickford.

3．埃德娜·库珀（Edna Cooper）

4．莉莲·吉什（Lilian Gish）在大卫·瓦克·格菲思（David Wark Griffith）执导的影片《东方之路》中的剧照。1920年。

5、6、7．菲拉格慕为玛丽·碧克馥（Mary Pickford）设计的两款鞋履模型。

8, 9. Gold kid shoe created in 1924 for Douglas Fairbanks in the movie *The Thief of Baghdad*, directed by Raoul Walsh.

8、9. 1924年为道格拉斯·费尔班克斯（Douglas Fairbanks）出演拉乌尔·沃尔什（Raoul Walsh）执导的影片《巴格达大盗》所设计的金色小山羊皮面料皮鞋。

9

8

10. Salvatore Ferragamo with the lasts made for his famous customers. 1955.

11, 12. Blue suede sandal. The model was made for Lana Turner in 1939 and reproduced for the movie *The Postman Rings Always Twice* by Tay Garnett in 1946.

13, 14. Brown calf shoe with cork wedge heel covered in green calf, made for Katharine Hepburn in 1942.

10．萨尔瓦托勒·菲拉格慕与他为著名顾客设计的鞋楦，1955年。

11、12．蓝色绒面革凉鞋。这一鞋款于1939年为拉娜·特纳（Lana Turner）设计，并于1946年为泰·加尼特（Tay Garnett）执导的影片《邮差总按两次铃》再次制作。

13、14．1942年为凯瑟琳·赫本（Katharine Hepburn）设计的褐色小牛皮面料皮鞋，软木楔形鞋跟，外包绿色小牛皮。

17. Marlene Dietrich
in the 1940s.

17．上世纪40年代的玛莲
娜·迪特里茜（Marlene
Dietrich）。

15. Greta Garbo and
Salvatore Ferragamo
in 1949.

16. *Attica* suede shoe
with cork wedge heel,
created for Greta Garbo
in 1942.

15．葛丽泰·嘉宝
（Greta Garbo）与萨
尔瓦托勒·菲拉格慕，
1949年。

16．"Attica"女鞋。
软木楔形鞋跟绒面革面
料凉鞋，于1942年为
葛丽泰·嘉宝（Greta
Garbo）设计。

18, 19. Sandal with raffia
upper and cork heel,
made for the actress
Loretta Young in 1940.

20, 21. *Ava* black silk
velvet sandal. The model
was made for Ava
Gardner in 1947.

18、19．1940年为女演
员洛丽塔·扬（Loretta
Young）设计的酒椰纤维
鞋帮软木鞋跟凉鞋。

20、21．"Ava"黑
色丝绒凉鞋。1947年
为艾娃·加德纳（Ava
Gardner）设计。

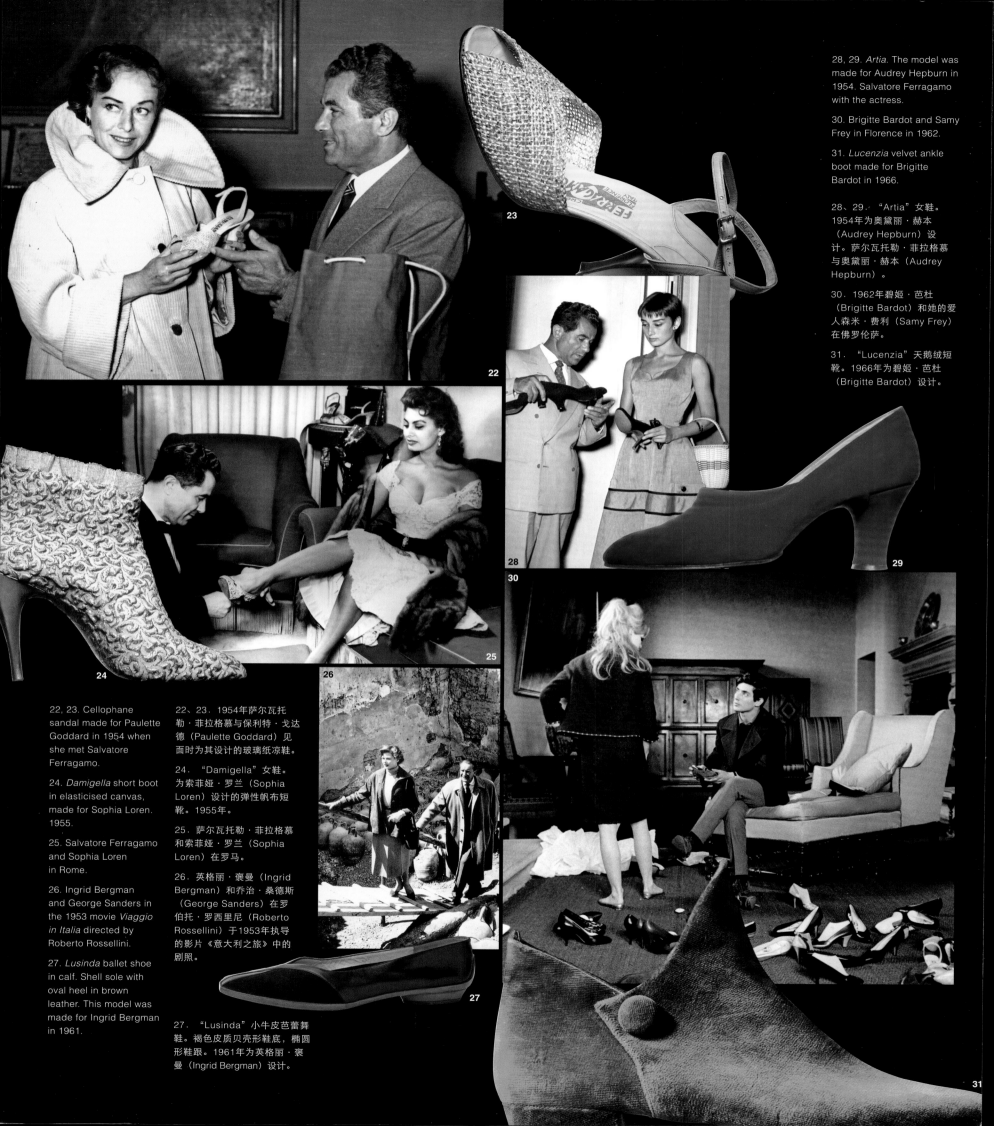

28, 29. *Artia*. The model was made for Audrey Hepburn in 1954. Salvatore Ferragamo with the actress.

30. Brigitte Bardot and Samy Frey in Florence in 1962.

31. *Lucenzia* velvet ankle boot made for Brigitte Bardot in 1966.

28、29． "Artia" 女鞋。1954年为奥黛丽·赫本 (Audrey Hepburn) 设计。萨尔瓦托勒·菲拉格慕与奥黛丽·赫本 (Audrey Hepburn)。

30． 1962年碧姬·芭杜 (Brigitte Bardot) 和她的爱人森米·费利 (Samy Frey) 在佛罗伦萨。

31． "Lucenzia" 天鹅绒短靴。1966年为碧姬·芭杜 (Brigitte Bardot) 设计。

22, 23. Cellophane sandal made for Paulette Goddard in 1954 when she met Salvatore Ferragamo.

24. *Damigella* short boot in elasticised canvas, made for Sophia Loren. 1955.

25. Salvatore Ferragamo and Sophia Loren in Rome.

26. Ingrid Bergman and George Sanders in the 1953 movie *Viaggio in Italia* directed by Roberto Rossellini.

27. *Lusinda* ballet shoe in calf. Shell sole with oval heel in brown leather. This model was made for Ingrid Bergman in 1961.

22、23． 1954年萨尔瓦托勒·菲拉格慕与保利特·戈达德 (Paulette Goddard) 见面时为其设计的玻璃纸凉鞋。

24． "Damigella" 女鞋。为索菲娅·罗兰 (Sophia Loren) 设计的弹性帆布短靴。1955年。

25． 萨尔瓦托勒·菲拉格慕和索菲娅·罗兰 (Sophia Loren) 在罗马。

26． 英格丽·褒曼 (Ingrid Bergman) 和乔治·桑德斯 (George Sanders) 在罗伯托·罗西里尼 (Roberto Rossellini) 于1953年执导的影片《意大利之旅》中的剧照。

27． "Lusinda" 小牛皮芭蕾舞鞋。褐色皮质贝壳形鞋底，椭圆形鞋跟。1961年为英格丽·褒曼 (Ingrid Bergman) 设计。

32, 33. Court-shoe
with upper covered with
red Swarovski, made
for Marilyn Monroe.
1959–60.

32、33．为玛丽莲·
梦露（Marilyn Monroe）
设计的无带高跟鞋，
鞋帮饰有红色施华洛世
奇（Swarovski）水晶，
1959-1960年。

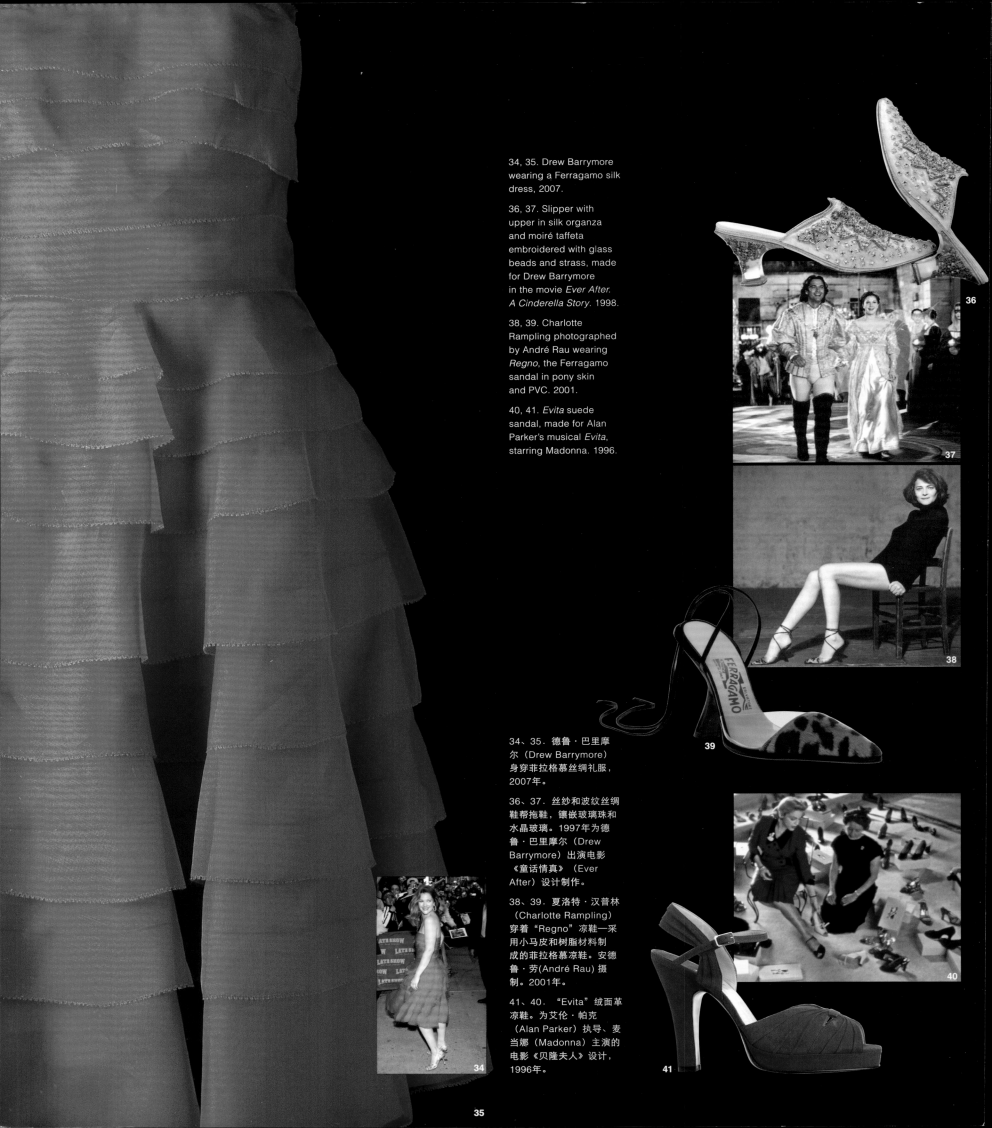

34, 35. Drew Barrymore wearing a Ferragamo silk dress, 2007.

36, 37. Slipper with upper in silk organza and moiré taffeta embroidered with glass beads and strass, made for Drew Barrymore in the movie *Ever After. A Cinderella Story*. 1998.

38, 39. Charlotte Rampling photographed by André Rau wearing *Regno*, the Ferragamo sandal in pony skin and PVC. 2001.

40, 41. *Evita* suede sandal, made for Alan Parker's musical *Evita*, starring Madonna. 1996.

34、35. 德鲁·巴里摩尔（Drew Barrymore）身穿菲拉格慕丝绸礼服，2007年。

36、37. 丝纱和波纹丝绸鞋帮拖鞋，镶嵌玻璃珠和水晶玻璃。1997年为德鲁·巴里摩尔（Drew Barrymore）出演电影《童话情真》（Ever After）设计制作。

38、39. 夏洛特·汉普林（Charlotte Rampling）穿着"Regno"凉鞋—采用小马皮和树脂材料制成的菲拉格慕凉鞋。安德鲁·劳(André Rau) 摄制。2001年。

41、40. "Evita"绒面革凉鞋。为艾伦·帕克（Alan Parker）执导、麦当娜（Madonna）主演的电影《贝隆夫人》设计，1996年。

36

37

38

39

40

41

34

47

48

49

50

51

52

42, 43. Embroidered satin sandal created for the Chinese actress Zhang Zi Yi in 2003. Zhang Zi Yi and James Ferragamo at Palazzo Spini Feroni, 2002.

44, 45. Sarah Jessica Parker and Eva Mendes with Ferragamo bags.

46. Catherine Zeta-Jones wearing a Ferragamo silk poncho. 2005.

47. Oxford shoe with hand-stitched welt in crocodile made for the Chinese actor Tony Leung. 2004.

48. Mel Gibson in a scene from Wim Wenders' *The Million Dollar Hotel.* He is wearing Ferragamo shoes.

49. Suit design for the Chinese director Wong Kar-Wai. 2007.

50, 51, 52. Two historical models created for Nicole Kidman in Baz Luhrmann's movie *Australia.*

pp. 188–89. Claudia Schiffer in the Ferragamo advertising campaign. Spring/Summer 2008.

42、43. 2003年为中国女影星章子怡设计的刺绣绸缎凉鞋。章子怡与詹姆士·菲拉格慕(James Ferragamo)在Palazzo Spini Feroni 菲拉格慕总部，2002年。

44、45. 莎拉·杰西卡·帕克（Sarah Jessica Parker）和艾娃·门德斯（Eva Mendes）携带着菲拉格慕包品。

46. 凯瑟琳·泽塔-琼斯（Catherine Zeta-Jones）身披菲拉格慕丝绸"斗篷"披肩，2005年。

47. 为中国男影星梁朝伟设计的牛津鞋，鳄鱼皮质地，饰有手工缝制滚边。2004年。

48. 梅尔·吉普森（Mel Gibson）在维姆·文德斯（Wim Wenders）执导的影片《百万大饭店》中的场景。他穿着菲拉格慕鞋履。

49. 为中国导演王家卫设计的西装，2007年。

50、51、52. 为妮可·基德曼（Nicole Kidman）出演巴兹·鲁赫曼（Baz Luhrmann）执导的影片《澳大利亚》设计的两款复古鞋履。

名模克劳迪娅·希夫（Claudia Schiffer）出席菲拉格慕广告宣传活动。2008春夏系列。

Bibliography / 参考书目

1957

Salvatore Ferragamo, *Shoemaker of Dreams. The Autobiography of Salvatore Ferragamo*, George G. Harrap & Co., London 1957 (last edition published by Sillabe, Livorno 2006; Chinese edition, Shanghai 2006).

1985

Kirsten Aschengreen Piacenti, Stefania Ricci and Guido Vergani, *I protagonisti della Moda / Leaders of Fashion. Salvatore Ferragamo*, exhibition catalogue (Florence, Palazzo Strozzi), Centro Di, Florence 1985.

1987

Roy Strong, Kirsten Aschengreen Piacenti, Valerie Mendes and Stefania Ricci, *Salvatore Ferragamo. The Art of the Shoe*, exhibition catalogue (London, Victoria & Albert Museum), Salvatore Ferragamo Italia, Florence 1987.

1992

Earl A. Powell, Kirsten Aschengreen Piacenti, Edward Maeder and Stefania Ricci, *Salvatore Ferragamo. The Art of the Shoe*, exhibition catalogue (Los Angeles County Museum of Art), Rizzoli International Publications, New York 1992.

1995

Stefania Ricci (ed.), *Palazzo Spini Feroni and its Museum*, Giorgio Mondadori, Florence 1995.

1997

Stefania Ricci (ed.), *Materials and Creativity*, exhibition catalogue (Florence, Salvatore Ferragamo Museum), Salvatore Ferragamo Italia, Florence 1997.

1998

Stefania Ricci, *Salvatore Ferragamo. The Art of the Shoe*, exhibition catalogue (Tokyo, Sogetzu Kai Foundation), Kodansha Publishers, Tokyo 1998.

1999

Stefania Ricci (ed.), *Audrey Hepburn. A Woman, The Style*, exhibition catalogue (Florence, Salvatore Ferragamo Museum), Leonardo Arte, Milan 1999.

2000

Stefania Ricci (ed.), *Scarpe e piedi famosi / Shoes and Famous Feet*, exhibition catalogue (Florence, Salvatore Ferragamo Museum), Leonardo Arte, Milan 2000.

Stefania Ricci, *L'isola della seta / The Isle of Silk*, Leonardo Arte, Milan 2000.

François Baudot, *Salvatore Ferragamo*, Assouline, Paris 2000.

2004

Stefania Ricci, *A Love Affair with Shoes*, Sillabe, Livorno 2004.

Stefania Ricci (ed.), *Idee, modelli, invenzioni / Ideas, Models, Inventions*, exhibition catalogue (Florence, Salvatore Ferragamo Museum), Sillabe, Livorno 2004.

2006

Stefania Ricci (ed.), *Creatività a colori / Creativity in Colour*, exhibition catalogue (Florence, Salvatore Ferragamo Museum), Sillabe, Livorno 2006.

Stefania Ricci (ed.), *Walking Dreams*, exhibition catalogue (Mexico City, Museo del Palacio de Bellas Artes), Editorial RM, Mexico City 2006.

2007

Amin Jaffer, *The Amazing World of Maharajah*, White Star Edition, Vercelli 2007.

1957年

萨尔瓦托勒·菲拉格慕著
《梦鞋匠》—萨尔瓦托勒·菲拉格慕自传
1957年由伦敦George G. Harrap & Co.出版（最后一版由意大利里窝那Sillabe出版，2006年）
中文版由上海画报出版社出版，2006年

1985年

Kirsten Aschengreen Piacenti、Stefania Ricci、Guido Vergani合著
《I protagonisti della Moda／萨尔瓦托勒·菲拉格慕，时尚先驱》
展览目录—佛罗伦萨斯特罗兹宫
佛罗伦萨Centro Di

1987年

Roy Strong、Kirsten Aschengreen Piacenti、Valerie Mendes、Stefania Ricci合著
《萨尔瓦托勒·菲拉格慕：制鞋艺术》
展览目录—维多利亚与艾伯特博物馆
意大利佛罗伦萨萨尔瓦托勒·菲拉格慕公司出版

1992年

Earl A. Powell、Kirsten Aschengreen Piacenti、Edward Maeder、Stefania Ricci合著
《萨尔瓦托勒·菲拉格慕：制鞋艺术》
展览目录—洛杉矶艺术博物馆
纽约Rizzoli International Publications出版

1995年

Stefania Ricci编著
《Palazzo Spini Feroni及其博物馆》
佛罗伦萨Giorgio Mondadori出版

1997年

Stefania Ricci编著
《选料与创造性》
展览目录—佛罗伦萨萨尔瓦托勒·菲拉格慕博物馆
佛罗伦萨萨尔瓦托勒·菲拉格慕博物馆出版

1998年

Stefania Ricci著
《萨尔瓦托勒·菲拉格慕：制鞋艺术》
展览目录—东京Sogetzu Kai Foundation
东京Kodansha Publishers出版

1999年

Stefania Ricci编著
《奥黛丽·赫本—女人与优雅合一》
展览目录—佛罗伦萨萨尔瓦托勒·菲拉格慕博物馆
米兰Leonardo Arte出版

2000年

Stefania Ricci编著
《名人与名鞋》
展览目录—佛罗伦萨萨尔瓦托勒·菲拉格慕博物馆
米兰Leonardo Arte出版

Stefania Ricci著
《丝绸之岛》
米兰Leonardo Arte出版

Francois Baudot著
《萨尔瓦托勒·菲拉格慕》
巴黎Assouline出版

2004年

Stefania Ricci著
《鞋之恋》
里窝那Sillabe出版

Stefania Ricci编著
《构思、制模、创作》
展览目录—佛罗伦萨萨尔瓦托勒·菲拉格慕博物馆
里窝那Sillabe出版

2006年

Stefania Ricci编著
《色彩的创造力》
展览目录—佛罗伦萨萨尔瓦托勒·菲拉格慕博物馆
里窝那Sillabe出版

Stefania Ricci编著
《永远的梦》
展览目录—墨西哥城Museo Del Palacio de Bellas Artes
墨西哥城Editorial RM出版

2007年

Amin Jaffer著
《Maharajah迷人的世界》
维切利White Star Edition出版